Henry Morley

Famous Pamphlets

Henry Morley

Famous Pamphlets

ISBN/EAN: 9783337073206

Printed in Europe, USA, Canada, Australia, Japan

Cover: Foto ©Thomas Meinert / pixelio.de

More available books at **www.hansebooks.com**

FAMOUS PAMPHLETS

MILTON'S
AREOPAGITICA

KILLING NO MURDER

DE FOË'S
SHORTEST WAY WITH THE DISSENTERS

STEELE'S
CRISIS

WHATELY'S
HISTORIC DOUBTS CONCERNING NAPOLEON BUONAPARTE

COPLESTON'S
ADVICE TO A YOUNG REVIEWER

WITH AN INTRODUCTION BY HENRY MORLEY
LL.D., PROFESSOR OF ENGLISH LITERATURE AT
UNIVERSITY COLLEGE, LONDON

LONDON
GEORGE ROUTLEDGE AND SONS
BROADWAY, LUDGATE HILL
NEW YORK: 9 LAFAYETTE PLACE
1886

MORLEY'S UNIVERSAL LIBRARY.

1. *Sheridan's Plays.*
2. *Plays from Molière.* By English Dramatists.
3. *Marlowe's Faustus* and *Goethe's Faust.*
4. *Chronicle of the Cid.*
5. *Rabelais' Gargantua* and the *Heroic Deeds of Pantagruel.*
6. *Machiavelli's Prince.*
7. *Bacon's Essays.*
8. *Defoe's Journal of the Plague Year.*
9. *Locke on Civil Government* and *Filmer's "Patriarcha."*
10. *Butler's Analogy of Religion.*
11. *Dryden's Virgil.*
12. *Scott's Demonology and Witchcraft.*
13. *Herrick's Hesperides.*
14. *Coleridge's Table-Talk.*
15. *Boccaccio's Decameron.*
16. *Sterne's Tristram Shandy.*
17. *Chapman's Homer's Iliad.*
18. *Mediæval Tales.*
19. *Voltaire's Candide,* and *Johnson's Rasselas.*
20. *Jonson's Plays and Poems.*
21. *Hobbes's Leviathan.*
22. *Samuel Butler's Hudibras.*
23. *Ideal Commonwealths.*
24. *Cavendish's Life of Wolsey.*
25 & 26. *Don Quixote.*
27. *Burlesque Plays and Poems.*
28. *Dante's Divine Comedy.* LONGFELLOW's Translation.
29. *Goldsmith's Vicar of Wakefield, Plays, and Poems.*
30. *Fables and Proverbs from the Sanskrit.* (*Hitopadesa.*)
31. *Lamb's Essays of Elia.*
32. *The History of Thomas Ellwood.*
33. *Emerson's Essays, &c.*
34. *Southey's Life of Nelson.*
35. *De Quincey's Confessions of an Opium-Eater, &c.*
36. *Stories of Ireland.* By Miss EDGEWORTH.
37. *Frere's Aristophanes: Acharnians, Knights, Birds.*
38. *Speeches and Letters by Edmund Burke.*
39. *Thomas à Kempis.*
40. *Popular Songs of Ireland.*
41. *The Plays of Æschylus.* POTTER's Translation.
42. *Goethe's Faust: Part II.* ANSTER's Translation.
43. *Famous Pamphlets.*

"Marvels of clear type and general neatness."—*Daily Telegraph.*

INTRODUCTION.

THE man who has something to say, and says it in as many words as are necessary to the clear, full and emphatic expression of his thought, must often be unable, without help of tedious impertinences, to spread it in ink over one or two pounds' weight of paper. The weightiest intellectual contribution to the study of some living question may possibly require for its true utterance not more than a dozen or two of printed leaves. Waste words are for some idle brain. Our modern Reviews and Magazines are, in one sense, a device for the collection of short pamphlets worth diffusion into volumes that have such currency as to assure their being widely read, and kept on record. Before there were Reviews established for such periodical collection each pamphlet came alone into the world, and in the days of the first famous pamphlet in this volume, Milton's Areopagitica, burning questions of the day that would now be argued out in leading articles and in reviews, were discussed by pamphlets in which every man fought for himself his battle of opinion, to be answered in pamphlets of opponents, and to be replied to in new pamphlets, until each question of truth and error had lain long enough in the sieve to be thoroughly sifted by the to and fro of opposite opinions. Sometimes, as in the old Church controversy between Whitgift and Cartwright, strong feeling and the wide stretch of the question caused these pamphlets of attack, reply, rejoinder to the reply, &c., to extend to the form of massive folios, heavy enough to knock down an antagonist if thrown as solid paper at his head. But though there was quick fencing with these folios, and they were produced as promptly as if they had been pamphlets in bulk as they were pamphlets in essence, they were technically volumes.

Why a work produced only upon a few leaves was called a pamphlet, it is hard to say with any certainty. Some say it was so called from the French *paume* and *feuillet*, as a leaf held in the hand. Others say that it was from a woman named Pamphila, who lived about eighteen hundred years ago and wrote many epitomes; others go for the source of the word to Spanish.

The most famous pamphlet in our language, and, considering its whole aim and the grandeur of some passages, the noblest piece of English prose, is that which stands first in this collection, John Milton's "Areopagitica: A Speech for the Liberty of Unlicensed Printing, to the Parliament of England." Henry VIII., when he destroyed the Pope's authority in England, took it to himself. He continued the censorship of books, which had been established for the suppression of opinions hostile to the established faith, and extended censorship over political writings which had not been checked by Rome. Queen Elizabeth allowed printing only to a few known presses in London, Oxford and Cambridge, and that was not the liberty of printing, for there was strict endeavour to suppress utterance of opinion that might disturb the order of the State. A decree of the Star Chamber, in 1637, limited the number of printers in the whole country to twenty and of type-founders to four, with provision for strict censorship of all they uttered to the world. In 1640 the Star Chamber was abolished, but in 1643, on the 14th of June, the Parliament adopted the same policy of suppression, by an Ordinance for the regulating of printing. Milton at once set himself to reason with the chiefs of his own party, and used all the force of his genius to make them understand that truth can be established only by the freest interchange of thought. The principle for which he contended is that upon which all healthy growth and national prosperity, in its true sense, must depend. He took for his model an oration written to be read, which was addressed by Isocrates to the Areopagus, the Great Council of Athens, and is known as the Areopagitic Discourse. Isocrates called on the Parliament of Athens to undo acts of its own; Milton was making a like call on the Areopagus of England. He gave to his work the exact form of a Greek oration, with exordium, statement, proof and peroration; and he put into it the very soul of England, claiming freedom in the search for truth. It was published in November 1644.

The next pamphlet in this collection, "Killing No Murder," was published in 1657, and is, perhaps, in our political literature, the most famous example of free utterance of free opinion, for it was a direct incitement to the assassination of Oliver Cromwell. It professed upon its title-page to be by William Allen, but its real author seems to have been the Colonel Sexby, a leveller, who had gone over to the Royalists, and in 1656, having come from Flanders to shoot Cromwell, joined the Protector's escort in Hyde Park and almost secured his opportunity. But he went back to Flanders, leaving sixteen hundred pounds of the money entrusted to him for such purposes with a cashiered quartermaster, Miles Sindercombe, who was to do the deed. Sindercombe took a house at Hammersmith in the narrow part of a road through which Cromwell often passed, and began by the shaping of a battery of seven blunderbusses. But difficulties came in his way. He resolved then to set fire to Whitehall and in the confusion to kill the Protector as he came out. A hundred swift horses were ready for changes to secure his escape. Many were aiding and abetting, and all was done with knowledge of the prince who ruled afterwards as Charles the Second. But the secret was shared by one too many. Henry Toope, a Life-guardsman, disclosed it. Sindercombe was arrested, tried, convicted, and sentenced to death, but took poison on the day before that which had been appointed for his execution. Then Sexby wrote and printed his pamphlet; himself travelling about England disguised as a country-man, with a large beard, to secure its distribution. He was after a time arrested and sent to the Tower, where he became mad and died within a year. After the Restoration, Colonel Titus claimed the honour of having written this pamphlet, and it was afterwards reprinted as his, with the doctrine of assassination freshly applied on the title-page to the French king.

Daniel De Foe's pamphlet, called the "The Shortest Way with the Dissenters," which comes next in this collection, was first published in 1702, at the beginning of Queen Anne's reign. The party that had no sympathy with the spirit of the English Revolution of 1688-89 then had a chance of power. There was a vigorous attack upon dissent, and a Bill had passed the House of Commons (but had been thrown out by the Lords) for disqualifying Dissenters from all civil employments. De Foe, bred a Dissenter, but as little in sympathy with the intolerance of one party as of the other, wrote with a fine irony in the character of a thorough-going Churchman, and argued the theory of persecution to its logical end in the impossible and the absurd. The reader will observe a curious resemblance between the style of argument in "Killing No Murder"—incitement to the assassination of a man—which was meant to be taken seriously, and that in "The Shortest Way with the Dissenters"—incitement to the assassination of a party—which was meant to be taken as satire. De Foe's treatment of intolerance brought him to prison and the pillory. For the writing of this pamphlet, he stood in the pillory on the three last days of July 1703, but by a Hymn to the Pillory dispersed among the people, he turned what was meant for his disgrace into a triumph, and transferred the contempt of the people to the men who placed him there.

For the next pamphlet in this volume, "The Crisis," a defender of English liberties not less in earnest than De Foe, the true-hearted Richard Steele, was expelled from the House of Commons at the end of Queen Anne's reign, on the 18th of March, 1714, by the same party that at the beginning of the reign had pilloried De Foe. There had been underhand dealings in aid of a second restoration of the Stuarts, and the settlement of the relations between Crown and people was in real danger during the last months of the reign of Queen Anne. Steele sought to secure what had been gained, and that in the simplest and directest way. Following the good suggestion of a lawyer that if the English people clearly knew what the Revolution meant they would be ready to defend it, he gave his literary skill and influence as a writer to the work of diffusing an exact knowledge of the latest title-deeds of English liberty. That he might present the documents without a thoughtless word of comment, he submitted proofs of his pamphlet to many foremost men, including his friend Addison, before its publication. The reader will find it so difficult to understand the bitterness of party feeling that wreaked its vengeance upon Steele for this calm endeavour to make their own recent history clearly known to the people, that we must suppose his opponents to have stopped their reading at the title-page. The somewhat sudden death of Queen Anne on the first of August next following, before plots were ripe, defeated expectations of reaction, and deprived Steele's adversaries of their power.

The next pamphlet in this volume—"Historic Doubts respecting Napoleon Buonaparte"—was written by Richard Whately, afterwards Archbishop of Dublin, and first published in 1819, three years after the Battle of Waterloo, and while Napoleon was still living in exile, for he died on the fifth of May 1821. Whately, born in 1787, was thirty-two years old when the pamphlet appeared. He had entered Oriel College, Oxford, in 1805, where Dr. Copleston, afterwards Dean of Chester and Bishop of Llandaff, was his tutor. Whately delighted in the teaching of Copleston, and Copleston in the earnest studies and clear wit of his pupil. Long afterwards Whately said that he remembered with a thrill of pleasure the first words of encouragement from his tutor's lips, "That is well, Mr. Whately: I see you understand it." In 1811 Whately was elected Fellow of Oriel. In 1812 he proceeded to the degree of M.A., and he was resident in Oriel as a tutor when he wrote this famous pamphlet, designed as a reduction to the absurd of the too sceptical spirit of inquiry.

Whately's tutor, Dr. Copleston, who was by eleven years his senior and had been elected to a Fellowship at Oriel in 1795, wrote also a famous little satirical pamphlet, the "Advice to a Young Reviewer," with which this volume closes. It was published at Oxford in 1807, and was designed as a reduction to the absurd of the censorious spirit of small critics. The great critics are not censorious.

H. M.

October 1886.

MILTON'S
AREOPAGITICA:

A DEFENCE OF THE LIBERTY OF UNLICENSED PRINTING.

AREOPAGITICA.

FOR THE LIBERTY OF UNLICENSED PRINTING.

THEY who to States and governors of the Commonwealth direct their speech, High Court of Parliament, or, wanting such access in a private condition, write that which they foresee may advance the public good, I suppose them, as at the beginning of no mean endeavour, not a little altered and moved inwardly in their minds: some with doubt of what will be the success, others with fear of what will be the censure; some with hope, others with confidence of what they have to speak. And me perhaps each of these dispositions, as the subject was whereon I entered, may have at other times variously affected; and likely might in these foremost expressions now also disclose which of them swayed most, but that the very attempt of this address thus made, and the thought of whom it hath recourse to, hath got the power within me to a passion, far more welcome than incidental to a preface. Which though I stay not to confess ere any ask, I shall be blameless, if it be no other than the joy and gratulation which it brings to all who wish and promote their country's liberty; whereof this whole discourse proposed will be a certain testimony, if not a trophy. For this is not the liberty which we can hope, that no grievance ever should arise in the Commonwealth, that let no man in this world expect; but when complaints are freely heard, deeply considered, and speedily reformed, then is the utmost bound of civil liberty attained that wise men look for. To which if I now manifest by the very sound of this which I shall utter that we are already in good part arrived, and yet from such a steep disadvantage of tyranny and superstition grounded into our principles as was beyond the manhood of a Roman recovery, it will be attributed first, as is most due, to the strong assistance of God our deliverer, next to your faithful guidance and undaunted wisdom, Lords and Commons of England. Neither, is it in God's esteem the diminution of his glory, when honourable things are spoken of good men and worthy magistrates; which if I now first should begin to do, after so fair a progress of your laudable deeds, and such a long obligement upon the whole realm to your indefatigable virtues, I might be justly reckoned among the tardiest and the unwillingest of them that praise ye. Nevertheless there being three principal things, without which all praising is but courtship and flattery, first, when that only is praised which is solidly worth praise: next, when greatest likelihoods are brought that such things are truly and really in those persons to whom they are ascribed: the other, when he who praises, by showing that such his actual persuasion is of whom he writes, can demonstrate that he flatters not; the former two of these I have heretofore endeavoured, rescuing the employment from him who went about to impair your merits with a trivial and malignant encomium; the latter as belonging chiefly to mine own acquittal, that whom I so extolled I did not flatter, hath been reserved opportunely to this occasion. For he who freely magnifies what hath been nobly done, and fears not to declare as freely what might be done better, gives ye the best covenant of his fidelity, and that his loyalest affection and his hope waits on your proceedings. His highest praising is not flattery, and his plainest advice is a kind of praising; for though I should affirm and hold by argument, that it would fare better with truth, with learning, and the Commonwealth, if one of your published orders, which I should name, were called in, yet at the same time it could not but much redound to the lustre of your mild and equal Government, when as private persons are hereby animated to think ye better pleased with public advice than other statists have been delighted heretofore with public flattery. And men will then see what difference there is between the magnanimity of a triennial Parliament and that jealous haughtiness of prelates and cabin counsellors that usurped of late, when as they shall observe ye in the midst of your victories and successes more gently brooking written exceptions against a voted order than other Courts, which had produced nothing worth memory but the weak ostentation of wealth, would have endured the least signified dislike at any sudden proclamation. If I should thus far presume upon the meek demeanour of your civil and gentle greatness, Lords and Commons, as what your published order hath directly said, that to gainsay, I might defend myself with ease, if any should accuse me of being new or insolent, did they but know how much better I find ye esteem it to imitate the old and elegant humanity of Greece than the barbaric pride of a Hunnish and Norwegian stateliness. And out of those ages, to whose polite wisdom and letters we owe that we are not yet Goths and Jutlanders, I could name him who from his private house wrote that discourse to the Parliament of Athens, that persuades them to change the form of Democracy which was then established. Such honour was done in those days to men who professed the study of wisdom and eloquence, not only in their own country, but in other lands, that cities and seignories heard them gladly and with great respect, if they had aught in public to admonish the State. Thus did Dion Prusæus, a stranger and a private orator, counsel the Rhodians against a former edict: and I abound with other like examples, which to set here would be superfluous. But if from the industry of a life wholly dedicated to studious labours, and those natural endowments haply not the worst for two-and-fifty degrees of northern latitude, so much must be derogated as to count me not equal to any of those who had this privilege, I would obtain to be thought not so inferior as yourselves are superior to the most of them who received their counsel: and how far you excel them, be assured, Lords and Commons, there can no greater testimony appear than when your prudent spirit acknowledges and obeys the voice of reason from what quarter soever it be heard speaking; and renders ye as willing to repeal any act of your own setting forth as any set forth by your predecessors.

If ye be thus resolved, as it were injury to think ye were not, I know not what should withhold me from presenting ye with a fit instance wherein to show both that love of truth which ye eminently profess, and that uprightness of your judgment which is not wont to be partial to yourselves, by judging over again that order which ye have ordained "to regulate printing: that no book, pamphlet, or paper shall be henceforth printed, unless the same be first approved and licensed by such," or at least one of such as shall be thereto appointed. For that part which preserves justly every man's copy to himself, or provides for the poor, I touch not, only wish they be not made pretences to abuse and persecute honest and painful men, who offend not in either of these particulars. But that other clause of Licensing Books, which we thought had died with his brother quadragesimal and matrimonial when the prelates expired, I shall now attend with such a homily as shall lay before ye, first the inventors of it to be those whom ye will be loth to own; next, what is to be thought in general of reading, whatever sort the books be; and that this order avails nothing to the suppressing of scandalous, seditious, and libellous books, which were mainly intended to be suppressed; last, that it will be primely to the discouragement of all learning and the stop of truth, not only by the disexercising and blunting our abilities in what we know already, but by hindering and cropping the discovery that might be yet further made both in religious and civil wisdom.

I deny not but that it is of greatest concernment in the Church and Commonwealth to have a vigilant eye how books demean themselves as well as men; and thereafter to confine, imprison, and do sharpest justice on them as malefactors: for books are not absolutely dead things, but do contain a potency of life in them to be as active as that soul was whose progeny they are; nay, they do preserve as in a vial the purest efficacy and extraction of that living intellect that bred them. I know they are as lively, and as vigorously productive, as those fabulous dragons' teeth; and, being sown up and down, may chance to spring up armed men. And yet on the other hand, unless wariness be used, as good almost kill a man as kill a good book; who kills a man kills a reasonable creature, God's image; but he who destroys a good book kills reason itself, kills the image of God as it were in the eye. Many a man lives a burden to the earth; but a good book is the precious life-blood of a master spirit, embalmed and treasured up on purpose to a life beyond life. 'Tis true, no age can restore a life, whereof perhaps there is no great loss; and revolutions of ages do not oft recover the loss of a rejected truth, for the want of which whole nations fare the worse. We should be wary therefore what persecution we raise against the living labours of public men, how we spill that seasoned life of man preserved and stored up in books; since we see a kind of homicide may be thus committed, sometimes a martyrdom, and, if it extend to the whole impression, a kind of massacre, whereof the execution ends not in the slaying of an elemental life, but strikes at that ethereal and fifth essence, the breath of reason itself, slays an immortality rather than a life. But lest I should be condemned of introducing licence while I oppose licensing, I refuse not the pains to be so much historical as will serve to show what hath been done by ancient and famous Commonwealths against this disorder, till the very time that this project of licensing crept out of the Inquisition, was caught up by our Prelates, and hath caught some of our Presbyters.

In Athens, where books and wits were ever busier than in any other part of Greece, I find but only two sorts of writings which the magistrate cared to take notice of: those either blasphemous and atheistical, or libellous. Thus the books of Protagoras were by the judges of Areopagus commanded to be burnt, and himself banished the territory, for a discourse begun with his confessing not to know "whether there were gods, or whether not." And against defaming, it was decreed that none should be traduced by name, as was the manner of Vetus Comœdia, whereby we may guess how they censured libelling; and this course was quick enough, as Cicero writes, to quell both the desperate wits of other atheists, and the open way of defaming, as the event showed. Of other sects and opinions, though tending to voluptuousness and the denying of Divine Providence, they took no heed. Therefore, we do not read that either Epicurus, or that libertine school of Cyrene, or what the Cynic impudence uttered, was ever questioned by the laws. Neither is it recorded that the writings of those old comedians were suppressed, though the acting of them were forbid; and that Plato commended the reading of Aristophanes, the loosest of them all, to his royal scholar Dionysius, is commonly known, and may be excused, if holy Chrysostom, as is reported, nightly studied so much the same author, and had the art to cleanse a scurrilous vehemence into the style of a rousing sermon. That other leading city of Greece, Lacedæmon, considering that Lycurgus their law-giver was so addicted to elegant learning as to have been the first that brought out of Ionia the scattered works of Homer, and sent the poet Thales from Crete to prepare and mollify the Spartan surliness with his smooth songs and odes, the better to plant among them law and civility, it is to be wondered how museless and unbookish they were, minding nought but the feats of war. There needed no licensing of books among them, for they disliked all but their own laconic apophthegms, and took a slight occasion to chase Archilochus out of their city, perhaps for composing in a higher strain than their own soldierly ballads and roundels could reach to; or if it were for his broad verses, they were not therein so cautious but they were as dissolute in their promiscuous conversing; whence Euripides affirms, in "Andromache," that their women were all unchaste. Thus much may give us light after what sort books were prohibited among the Greeks. The Romans also, for many ages trained up only to a military roughness, resembling most of the Lacedæmonian guise, knew of learning little but what their twelve tables and the Pontific College with their augurs and flamens taught them in religion and law, so unacquainted with other learning that when Carneades and Critolaus, with the Stoic Diogenes, coming ambassadors to Rome, took thereby occasion to give the city a taste of their philosophy, they were suspected for seducers by no less a man than Cato the Censor, who moved it in the Senate to dismiss them speedily, and to banish all such Attic babblers out of Italy. But Scipio and others of the noblest senators withstood him and his old Sabine austerity; honoured and admired the men; and the Censor himself at last in his old age fell to the study of that whereof before he was so scrupulous. And yet at the same time Nævius and Plautus, the first Latin comedians, had filled the city with all the borrowed scenes of Menander and Philemon. Then began to be considered there also what was to be done to libellous books and authors; for Nævius was quickly cast into prison for his unbridled pen, and released by the Tribunes upon his recantation. We read also that libels were burnt, and the makers punished by Augustus. The like severity no doubt was used if aught were impiously written against their esteemed gods. Except in these two points, how the world went in books the magistrate kept no reckoning. And therefore Lucretius without impeachment versifies his epicurism to Memmius, and had the honour to be set forth the second time by Cicero so great a father of the Commonwealth, although himself disputes against that opinion in his own writings. Nor was the satirical sharpness or naked plainness of Lucilius, or Catullus, or Flaccus, by any order prohibited. And for matters of State, the story of Titius Livius, though it extolled that part which Pompey held, was not therefore suppressed by Octavius Cæsar of the other faction. But that Naso was by him banished in his old age for the wanton poems of his youth was but a mere covert of State over some secret cause; and besides, the books were neither banished nor called in. From hence we shall meet with little else but tyranny in the Roman Empire, that we may not marvel if not so often bad as good books were silenced. I shall therefore deem to have been large enough in producing what among the ancients was punishable to write, save only which, all other arguments were free to treat on.

By this time the Emperors were become Christians, whose discipline in this point I do not find to have been more severe than what was formerly in practice. The books of those whom they took to be grand heretics were examined, refuted, and condemned in the General Councils; and not till then were prohibited, or burnt by authority of the Emperor. As for the writings of heathen authors, unless they were plain invectives against Christianity, as those of Porphyrius and Proclus, they met with no interdict that can be cited till about the year 400 in a Carthaginian Council, wherein Bishops themselves were forbid to read the books of Gentiles, but heresies they might read: while others long before them on the contrary scrupled more the books of heretics than of Gentiles. And that the primitive Councils and Bishops were wont only to declare what books were not commendable, passing no further, but leaving it to each one's conscience to read or to lay by, till after the year 800, is observed already by Padre Paolo, the great unmasker of the Trentine Council. After which time the Popes of Rome, engrossing what they pleased of political rule into their own hands, extended their dominion over men's eyes, as they had before over their judgments, burning and prohibiting to be read what they fancied not; yet sparing in their censures, and the books not many which they so dealt with, till Martin the Fifth by his Bull not only prohibited, but was the first that excommunicated the reading of heretical books; for about that time Wyclif and Huss growing terrible, were they who first drove the Papal Court to a stricter policy of prohibiting; which course Leo the Tenth and his successors followed, until the Council of Trent and the Spanish Inquisition engendering together brought forth or perfected those catalogues and expurging indexes that rake through the entrails of many an old good author with a violation worse than any could be offered to his tomb. Nor did they stay in matters heretical, but any subject that was not to their palate they either condemned in a prohibition, or had it straight into the new purgatory of an Index. To fill up the measure of encroachment, their last invention was to ordain that no book, pamphlet, or paper should be printed (as if St. Peter had bequeathed them the keys of the Press also out of Paradise) unless it were approved and licensed under the hands of two or three glutton friars. For example:

Let the Chancellor Cini be pleased to see if in this present work be contained aught that may withstand the printing.

VINCENT RABATTA,
Vicar of Florence.

I have seen this present work, and find nothing athwart the Catholic faith and good manners. In witness whereof I have given, &c.

NICOLO CINI,
Chancellor of Florence.

Attending the precedent relation, it is allowed that this present work of Davanzati may be printed.

VINCENT RABATTA, &c.

It may be printed, July 15.

Friar SIMON MOMPEI D'AMELIA,
Chancellor of the Holy Office in Florence.

Sure they have a conceit, if he of the bottomless pit had not long since broke prison, that this quadruple exorcism would bar him down. I fear their next design will be to get into their custody the licensing of that which they say Claudius intended, but went not through with. Vouchsafe to see another of their forms, the Roman stamp:

Imprimatur. If it seem good to the reverend Master of the Holy Palace.

BELCASTRO,
Viceregent.

Imprimatur.

Friar NICOLO RODOLFI, Master of the Holy Palace.

Sometimes five Imprimaturs are seen together dialoguewise in the piazza of one title-page, complimenting and ducking each to other with their shaven reverences, whether the author, who stands by in perplexity at the foot of his epistle, shall to the press or to the sponge. These are the pretty responsories, these are the dear antiphonies that so bewitched of late our prelates and their chaplains with the goodly echo they made, and besotted us to the gay imitation of a lordly Imprimatur, one from Lambeth House, another from the west end of Paul's; so apishly Romanizing that the word of command still was set down in Latin, as if the learned grammatical pen that wrote it would cast no ink without Latin ; or perhaps, as they thought, because no vulgar tongue was worthy to express the pure conceit of an Imprimatur ; but rather, as I hope, for that our English, the language of men ever famous and foremost in the achievements of liberty, will not easily find servile letters enough to spell such a dictatory presumption English. And thus ye have the inventors and the original of book-licensing ripped up, and drawn as lineally as any pedigree. We have it not, that can be heard of, from any ancient State, or polity, or Church, nor by any statute left us by our ancestors, elder or later ; nor from the modern custom of any reformed city or church abroad ; but from the most antichristian Council, and the most tyrannous Inquisition that ever inquired. Till then books were ever as freely admitted into the world as any other birth ; the issue of the brain was no more stifled than the issue of the womb ; no envious Juno sat cross-legged over the nativity of any man's intellectual offspring ; but if it proved a monster, who denies but that it was justly burnt, or sunk into the sea ? But that a book, in worse condition than a peccant soul, should be to stand before a jury ere it be born to the world, and undergo yet in darkness the judgment of Radamanth and his colleagues, ere it can pass the ferry backward into light, was never heard before, till that mysterious iniquity, provoked and troubled at the first entrance of reformation, sought out new limboes and new hells wherein they might include our books also within the number of their damned. And this was the rare morsel so officiously snatched up and so ill-favouredly imitated by our inquisiturient bishops and the attendant minorites their chaplains. That ye like not now these most certain authors of this licensing order, and that all sinister intention was far distant from your thoughts when ye were importuned the passing it all men who know the integrity of your actions, and how ye honour truth, will clear ye readily.

But some will say, What though the inventors were bad, the thing for all that may be good? It may so; yet if that thing be no such deep invention but obvious, and easy for any man to light on, and yet best and wisest commonwealths through all ages and occasions have forborne to use it, and falsest seducers and oppressors of men were the first who took it up, and to no other purpose but to obstruct and hinder the first approach of reformation, I am of those who believe it will be a harder alchemy than Lullius ever knew, to sublimate any good use out of such an invention. Yet this only is what I request to gain from this reason, that it may be held a dangerous and suspicious fruit, as certainly it deserves, for the tree that bore it, until I can dissect one by one the properties it has. But I have first to finish as was propounded, what is to be thought in general of reading books, whatever sort they be, and whether be more the benefit or the harm that thence proceeds?

Not to insist upon the examples of Moses, Daniel, and Paul, who were skilful in all the learning of the Egyptians, Chaldeans, and Greeks, which could not probably be without reading their books of all sorts, in Paul especially, who thought it no defilement to insert into Holy Scripture the sentences of three Greek poets, and one of them a tragedian, the question was notwithstanding sometimes controverted among the primitive doctors, but with great odds on that side which affirmed it both lawful and profitable, as was then evidently perceived, when Julian the Apostate and subtlest enemy to our faith made a decree forbidding Christians the study of heathen learning; for, said he, they wound us with our own weapons, and with our own arts and sciences they overcome us. And, indeed, the Christians were put so to their shifts by this crafty means, and so much in danger to decline into all ignorance, that the two Apollinarii were fain, as a man may say, to coin all the seven liberal sciences out of the Bible, reducing it into divers forms of orations, poems, dialogues, even to the calculating of a new Christian grammar. But saith the historian Socrates: The providence of God provided better than the industry of Apollinarius and his son by taking away that illiterate law with the life of him who devised it. So great an injury they then held it to be deprived of Hellenic learning;

and thought it a persecution more undermining and secretly decaying the Church than the open cruelty of Decius or Dioclesian. And perhaps it was with the same politic drift that the Devil whipped St. Jerome in a lenten dream, for reading Cicero; or else it was a phantasm bred by the fever which had then seized him. For had an angel been his discipliner, unless it were for dwelling too much upon Ciceronianisms, and had chastised the reading, not the vanity, it had been plainly partial, first, to correct him for grave Cicero, and not for scurril Plautus whom he confesses to have been reading not long before, next, to correct him only, and let so many more ancient fathers wax old in those pleasant and florid studies without the lash of such a tutoring apparition; insomuch that Basil teaches how some good use may be made of "Margites," a sportful poem, not now extant, writ by Homer; and why not then of "Morgante," an Italian romance much to the same purpose? But if it be agreed we shall be tried by visions, there is a vision recorded by Eusebius far ancienter than this tale of Jerome to the nun Eustochium, and besides has nothing of a fever in it. Dionysius Alexandrinus was about the year 240 a person of great name in the Church for piety and learning, who had wont to avail himself much against heretics by being conversant in their books; until a certain Presbyter laid it scrupulously to his conscience, how he durst venture himself among those defiling volumes. The worthy man, loth to give offence, fell into a new debate with himself what was to be thought ; when suddenly a vision sent from God—it his is own epistle that so avers it—confirmed him in these words : " Read any books whatever come to thy hands, for thou art sufficient both to judge aright and to examine each matter." To this revelation he assented the sooner, as he confesses, because it was answerable to that of the Apostle to the Thessalonians : " Prove all things ; hold fast that which is good." And he might have added another remarkable saying of the same author: "To the pure all things are pure," not only meats and drinks, but all kind of knowledge whether of good or evil ; the knowledge cannot defile, nor consequently the books, if the will and conscience be not defiled. For books are as meats and viands are, some of good, some of evil substance ; and yet God in that unapocryphal vision said, without exception, " Rise, Peter, kill and eat," leaving the choice to each man's discretion. Wholesome meats to a vitiated stomach differ little or nothing from unwholesome ; and best books to a naughty mind are not unappliable to occasions of evil. Bad meats will scarce breed good nourishment in the healthiest concoction ; but herein the difference is of bad books, that they to a discreet and judicious reader serve in many respects to discover, to confute, to forewarn, and to illustrate. Whereof what better witness can ye expect I should produce than one of your own now sitting in Parliament, the chief of learned men reputed in this land, Mr. Selden, whose volume of natural and national laws proves, not only by great authorities brought together, but by exquisite reasons and theorems almost mathematically demonstrative, that all opinions, yea, errors, known, read, and collated, are of main service and assistance toward the speedy attainment of what is truest. I conceive, therefore, that when God did enlarge the universal diet of man's body, saving ever the rules of temperance, he then also, as before, left arbitrary the dieting and repasting of our minds; as wherein every mature man might have to exercise his own leading capacity. How great a virtue is temperance, how much of moment through the whole life of man! Yet God commits the managing so great a trust, without particular law or prescription, wholly to the demeanour of every grown man. And therefore, when He himself tabled the Jews from heaven, that omer which was every man's daily portion of manna is computed to have been more than might have well sufficed the heartiest feeder thrice as many meals. For those actions, which enter into a man rather than issue out of him and therefore defile not, God uses not to captivate under a perpetual childhood of prescription, but trusts him with the gift of reason to be his own chooser; there were but little work left for preaching, if law and compulsion should grow so fast upon those things which heretofore were governed only by exhortation. Solomon informs us that much reading is a weariness to the flesh; but neither he nor other inspired author tells us that such or such reading is unlawful: yet certainly had God thought good to limit us herein, it had been much more expedient to have told us what was unlawful than what was wearisome. As for the burning of those Ephesian books by St. Paul's converts, it is replied the books were magic, the Syriac so renders them. It was a private act, a voluntary act, and leaves us to a voluntary imitation; the men in remorse burnt those books which were their own; the magistrate by this example is not appointed; these men practised the books, another might perhaps have read them in some sort usefully. Good and evil we know in the field of this world grow up together almost inseparably; and the knowledge of good is so involved and interwoven with the knowledge of evil, and in so many cunning resemblances hardly to be discerned, that those confused seeds, which were imposed on Psyche as an incessant labour to cull out and sort asunder, were not more intermixed. It was from out the rind of one apple tasted that the knowledge of good and evil as two twins cleaving together leapt forth into the world. And perhaps this is that doom which Adam fell into of knowing good and evil, that is to say, of knowing good by evil. As therefore the state of man now is, what wisdom can there be to choose, what continence to forbear, without the knowledge of evil? He that can apprehend and consider vice with all her baits and seeming pleasures, and yet abstain, and yet distinguish, and yet prefer that which is truly better, he is the true warfaring Christian. I cannot praise a fugitive and cloistered virtue, unexercised and unbreathed, that never sallies out and sees her adversary, but slinks out of the race, where that immortal garland is to be run for not without dust and heat. Assuredly we bring not innocence into the world, we bring impurity much rather: that which purifies us is trial, and trial is by what is contrary. That virtue therefore which is but a youngling in the contemplation of evil, and knows not the utmost that vice promises to her followers, and rejects it, is but a blank virtue, not a pure; her whiteness is but an excremental whiteness; which was the reason why our sage and serious poet Spenser, whom I dare be known to think a better teacher then Scotus or Aquinas, describing true temperance under the person of Guyon, brings him in with his palmer through the cave of Mammon and the bower of earthly bliss, that he might see and know, and yet abstain. Since, therefore, the knowledge and survey of vice is in this world so necessary to the constituting of human virtue, and the scanning of error to the confirmation of truth, how can we more safely and with less danger scout into the regions of sin and falsity, than by reading all manner of tractates, and hearing all manner of reason? And this is the benefit which may be had of books promiscuously read. But of the harm that may result hence three kinds are usually reckoned: First, is feared the infection that may spread; but then all human learning and controversy in religious points must remove out of the world, yea, the Bible itself; for that ofttimes relates blasphemy not nicely, it describes the carnal sense of wicked men not unelegantly, it brings in holiest men passionately murmuring against Providence through all the arguments of Epicurus; in other great disputes it answers dubiously and darkly to the common reader: and ask a Talmudist what ails the modesty of his marginal Keri, that Moses and all the Prophets cannot persuade him to pronounce the textual Chetiv. For these causes we all know the Bible itself put by the Papist into the first rank of prohibited books. The ancientest Fathers must be next removed, as Clement of Alexandria, and that Eusebian book of Evangelic preparation, transmitting our ears through a hoard of heathenish obscenities to receive the Gospel. Who finds not that Irenæus, Epiphanius, Jerome, and others discover more heresies than they well confute, and that oft for heresy which is the truer opinion? Nor boots it to say for these, and all the heathen writers of greatest infection, if it must be thought so, with whom is bound up the life of human learning, that they wrote in an unknown tongue, so long as we are sure those languages are known as well to the worst of men, who are both most able and most diligent to instil the poison they suck, first into the Courts of Princes, acquainting them with the choicest delights and criticisms of sin : as perhaps did that Petronius whom Nero called his Arbiter, the master of his revels ; and that notorious ribald of Arezzo, dreaded, and yet dear to the Italian courtiers. I name not him, for posterity's sake, whom Harry the Eighth named in merriment his Vicar of Hell. By which compendious way all the contagion that foreign books can infuse will find a passage to the people far easier and shorter than an Indian voyage, though it could be sailed either by the north of Cathay eastward or of Canada westward, while our Spanish licensing gags the English press never so severely. But, on the other side, that infection which is from books of controversy in religion is more doubtful and dangerous to the learned than to the ignorant ; and yet those books must be permitted untouched by the licenser. It will be hard to instance where any ignorant man hath been ever seduced by Papistical book in English, unless it were commended and expounded to him by some of that clergy ; and indeed all such tractates, whether false or true, are as the prophecy of Isaiah was to the Eunuch, not to be "understood without a guide."

But of our priests and doctors how many have been corrupted by studying the comments of Jesuits and Sorbonnists, and how fast they could transfuse that corruption into the people our experience is both late and sad. It is not forgot since the acute and distinct Arminius was perverted merely by the perusing of a nameless discourse written at Delft, which at first he took in hand to confute. Seeing therefore that those books, and those in great abundance, which are likeliest to taint both life and doctrine, cannot be suppressed without the fall of learning and of all ability in disputation ; and that these books of either sort are most and soonest catching to the learned, from whom to the common people whatever is heretical or dissolute may quickly be conveyed ; and that evil manners are as perfectly learnt without books a thousand other ways which cannot be stopped, and evil doctrine not with books can propagate, except a teacher guide, which he might also do without writing and so beyond prohibiting, I am not able to unfold how this cautelous enterprise of licensing can be exempted from the number of vain and impossible attempts. And he who were pleasantly disposed could not well avoid to liken it to the exploit of that gallant man who thought to pound up the crows by shutting his park gate. Besides another inconvenience, if learned men be the first receivers out of books and dispreaders both of vice and error, how shall the licensers themselves be confided in, unless we can confer upon them, or they assume to themselves, above all others in the land, the grace of infallibility and uncorruptedness? And again, if it be true that a wise man like a good refiner can gather gold out of the drossiest volume, and that a fool will be a fool with the best book, yea, or without book, there is no reason that we should deprive a wise man of any advantage to his wisdom, while we seek to restrain from a fool that which being restrained will be no hindrance to his folly. For if there should be so much exactness always used to keep that from him which is unfit for his reading, we should, in the judgment of Aristotle not only, but of Solomon and of our Saviour, not vouchsafe him good precepts, and by consequence not willingly admit him to good books, as being certain that a wise man will make better use of an idle pamphlet than a fool will do of sacred Scripture. 'Tis next alleged we must not expose ourselves to temptations without necessity, and next to that, not employ our time in vain things. To both these objections one answer will serve, out of the grounds already laid, that to all men such books are not temptations nor vanities, but useful drugs and materials wherewith to temper and compose effective and strong medicines, which man's life cannot want. The rest, as children and childish men, who have not the art to qualify and prepare these working minerals, well may be exhorted to forbear, but hindered forcibly they cannot be by all the licensing that sainted Inquisition could ever yet contrive, which is what I promised to deliver next : that this order of licensing conduces nothing to the end for which it was framed, and hath almost prevented me by being clear already while thus much hath been explaining. See the ingenuity of Truth, who, when she gets a free and willing hand, opens herself faster than the pace of method and discourse can overtake her. It was the task which I began with, to show that no nation, or well instituted state, if they valued books at all, did ever use this way of licensing ; and it might be answered, that this is a piece of prudence lately discovered ; to which I return that, as it was a thing slight and obvious to think on, so if it had been difficult to find out there wanted not among them long since who suggested such a course, which they not following, leave us a pattern of their judgment, that it was not the not knowing, but the not approving, which was the cause of their not using it. Plato, a man of high authority indeed, but least of all for his Commonwealth, in the book of his laws, which no city ever yet received, fed his fancy with making many edicts to his airy burgomasters, which they who otherwise admire him wish had been rather buried and excused in the genial cups of an academic night-sitting ; by which laws he seems to tolerate no kind of learning but by unalterable decree, consisting most of practical traditions, to the attainment whereof a library of smaller bulk than his own Dialogues would be abundant. And there also enacts that no poet should so much as read to any private man what he had written, until the judges and law-keepers had seen it and allowed it. But that Plato meant this law peculiarly to that commonwealth which he had imagined, and to no other, is evident. Why was he not else a lawgiver to himself, but a transgressor, and to be expelled by his own magistrates, both for the wanton epigrams and dialogues which he made, and his perpetual reading of Sophron Mimus and Aristophanes, books of grossest infamy, and also for commending the latter of them, though he were the malicious libeller of his chief friends, to be read by the tyrant Dionysius, who had little need of such trash to spend his time on? But that he knew this licensing of poems had reference and dependence to many other provisoes there set down in his fancied republic, which in this world could have no place; and so neither he himself nor any magistrate or city ever imitated that course, which, taken apart from those other collateral injunctions, must needs be vain and fruitless. For if they fell upon one kind of strictness, unless their care were equal to regulate all other things of like aptness to corrupt the mind, that single endeavour they knew would be but a fond labour: to shut and fortify one gate against corruption, and be necessitated to leave others round about wide open. If we think to regulate printing, thereby to rectify manners, we must regulate all recreations and pastimes, all that is delightful to man. No music must be heard, no song be set or sung, but what is grave and Doric. There must be licensing dancers, that no gesture, motion, or deportment be taught our youth but what by their allowance shall be thought honest; for such Plato was provided of. It will ask more than the work of twenty licensers to examine all the lutes, the violins, and the guitars in every house; they must not be suffered to prattle as they do, but must be licensed what they may say. And who shall silence all the airs and madrigals, that whisper softness in chambers? The windows also, and the balconies, must be thought on: there are shrewd books with dangerous frontispieces set to sale; who shall prohibit them? Shall twenty licensers? The villages also must have their visitors to inquire what lectures the bagpipe and the rebec reads, even to the ballatry and the gamut of every municipal fiddler, for these are the countryman's Arcadias and his Montemayors. Next, what more national corruption, for which England hears ill abroad, than household gluttony? Who shall be the rectors of our daily rioting? and what shall be done to inhibit the multitudes that frequent those houses where drunkenness is sold and harboured? Our garments also should be referred to the licensing of some more sober work-masters to see them cut into a less wanton garb. Who shall regulate all the mixed conversation of our youth, male and female together, as is the fashion of this country? who shall still appoint what shall be discoursed, what presumed, and no further? Lastly, who shall forbid and separate all idle resort, all evil company? These things will be, and must be; but how they shall be less hurtful, how less enticing, herein consists the grave and governing wisdom of a State. To sequester out of the world into Atlantic and Utopian polities, which never can be drawn into use, will not mend our condition; but to ordain wisely as in this world of evil, in the midst whereof God hath placed us unavoidably. Nor is it Plato's licensing of books will do this, which necessarily pulls along with it so many other kinds of licensing, as will make us all both ridiculous and weary, and yet frustrate; but those unwritten, or at least unconstraining laws of virtuous education, religious and civil nurture, which Plato there mentions as the bonds and ligaments of the Commonwealth, the pillars and the sustainers of every written statute; these they be which will bear chief sway in such matters as these, when all licensing will be easily eluded. Impunity and remissness, for certain, are the bane of a Commonwealth; but here the great art lies to discern in what the law is to bid restraint and punishment, and in what things persuasion only is to work. If every action which is good or evil in man at ripe years, were to be under pittance and prescription and compulsion, what were virtue but a name, what praise could be then due to well-doing, what grammercy to be sober, just, or continent? Many there be that complain of Divine Providence for suffering Adam to transgress. Foolish tongues! When God gave him reason, He gave him freedom to choose, for reason is but choosing; he had been else a mere artificial Adam, such an Adam as he is in the motions. We ourselves esteem not of that obedience or love or gift which is of force: God therefore left him free, set before him a provoking object, ever almost in his eyes; herein consisted his merit, herein the right of his reward, the praise of his abstinence. Wherefore did He create passions within us, pleasures round about us, but that these rightly tempered are the very ingredients of virtue? They are not skilful considerers of human things who imagine to remove sin by removing the matter of sin; for, besides that it is a huge heap increasing under the very act of diminishing, though some part of it may for a time be withdrawn from some persons, it cannot from all in such a universal thing as books are; and when this is done, yet the sin remains entire. Though ye take from a covetous man all his treasure, he has yet one jewel left: ye cannot bereave him of his covetousness. Banish all objects of lust, shut up all youth into the severest discipline that can be exercised in any hermitage, ye cannot make them chaste that came not thither so; such great care and wisdom is required to the right managing of this point. Suppose we could expel sin by this means; look how much we thus expel of sin, so much we expel of virtue: for the matter of them both is the same; remove that, and ye remove them both alike. This justifies the high providence of God, who though He command us temperance, justice, continence, yet pours out before us even to a profuseness all desirable things, and gives us minds that can wander beyond all limit and satiety. Why should we then affect a rigour contrary to the manner of God and of Nature, by abridging or scanting those means which books freely permitted are, both to the trial of virtue and the exercise of truth. It would be better done to learn that the law must needs be frivolous which goes to restrain things uncertainly and yet equally working to good and to evil. And were I the chooser, a dram of well-doing should be preferred before many times as much the forcible hindrance of evil-doing. For God sure esteems the growth and completing of one virtuous person more than the restraint of ten vicious. And albeit whatever thing we hear or see, sitting, walking, travelling, or conversing, may be fitly called our book, and is of the same effect that writings are, yet grant the thing to be prohibited were only books, it appears that this order hitherto is far insufficient to the end which it intends. Do we not see, not once or oftener, but weekly that continued Court-libel against the Parliament and City, printed, as the wet sheets can witness, and dispersed among us for all that licensing can do? Yet this is the prime service a man would think, wherein this order should give proof of itself. If it were executed, you'll say. But certain, if execution be remiss or blindfold now and in this particular, what will it be hereafter and in other books? If then the order shall not be vain and frustrate, behold a new labour, Lords and Commons! Ye must repeal and proscribe all scandalous and unlicensed books already printed and divulged, after ye have drawn them up into a list, that all may know which are condemned and which not, and ordain that no foreign books be delivered out of custody till they have been read over. This office will require the whole time of not a few overseers, and those no vulgar men. There be also books which are partly useful and excellent, partly culpable and pernicious; this work will ask as many more officials to make expurgations and expunctions, that the commonwealth of learning be not damnified. In fine, when the multitude of books increase upon their hands. ye must be fain to catalogue all those printers who are found frequently offending, and forbid the importation of their whole suspected typography. In a word, that this your order may be exact, and not deficient, ye must reform it perfectly according to the model of Trent and Seville, which I know ye abhor to do. Yet though ye should condescend to this, which God forbid, the order still would be but fruitless and defective to that end whereto ye meant it. If to prevent sects and schisms, who is so unread or so uncatechized in story, that hath not heard of many sects refusing books as a hindrance, and preserving their doctrine unmixed for many ages only by unwritten traditions? The Christian faith, for that was once a schism, is not unknown to have spread all over Asia ere any Gospel or Epistle was seen in writing. If the amendment of manners be aimed at, look into Italy and Spain, whether those places be one scruple the better, the honester, the wiser, the chaster, since all the inquisitional rigour that hath been executed upon books.

Another reason, whereby to make it plain that this order will miss the end it seeks, consider by the quality which ought to be in every licenser. It cannot be denied but that he who is made judge to sit upon the birth or death of books, whether they may be wafted into this world or not, had need to be a man above the common measure, both studious, learned, and judicious; there may be else no mean mistakes in the censure of what is passable or not, which is also no mean injury. If he be of such worth as behoves him, there cannot be a more tedious and unpleasing journey-work, a greater loss of time levied upon his head, than to be made the perpetual reader of unchosen books and pamphlets, ofttimes huge volumes. There is no book that is acceptable unless at certain seasons; but to be enjoined the reading of that at all times, and in a hand scarce legible, whereof three pages would not down at any time in the fairest print, is an imposition which I cannot believe how he that values time and his own studies, or is but of a sensible nostril, should be able to endure. In this one thing I crave leave of the present licensers to be pardoned for so thinking, who doubtless took this office up looking on it through their obedience to the Parliament, whose command perhaps made all things seem easy and unlaborious to them; but that this short trial hath wearied them out already, their own expressions and excuses to them who make so many journeys to solicit their licence are testimony enough. Seeing therefore those who now possess the employment by all evident signs wish themselves well rid of it, and that no man of worth, none that is not a plain unthrift of his own hours, is ever likely to succeed them, except he mean to put himself to the salary of a press correcter, we may easily foresee what kind of licensers we are to expect hereafter, either ignorant, imperious, and remiss, or basely pecuniary. This is what I had to show wherein this order cannot conduce to that end whereof it bears the intention.

I lastly proceed from the no good it can do to the manifest hurt it causes, in being first the greatest discouragement and affront that can be offered to learning and to learned men. It was the complaint and lamentation of prelates upon every least breath of a motion to remove pluralities and distribute more equally Church revenues, that then all learning would be for ever dashed and discouraged. But as for that opinion, I never found cause to think that the tenth part of learning stood or fell with the clergy, nor could I ever but hold it for a sordid and unworthy speech of any churchman who had a competency left him. If, therefore, ye be loth to dishearten utterly and discontent, not the mercenary crew of false pretenders to learning, but the free and ingenuous sort of such as evidently were born to study and love learning for itself, not for lucre or any other end but the service of God and of truth, and perhaps that lasting fame and perpetuity of praise which God and good men have consented shall be the reward of those whose published labours advance the good of mankind, then know, that so far to distrust the judgment and the honesty of one who hath but a common repute in learning and never yet offended, as not to count him fit to print his mind without a tutor and examiner, lest he should drop a schism or something of corruption, is the greatest displeasure and indignity to a free and knowing spirit that can be put upon him. What advantage is it to be a man over it is to be a boy at school, if we have only escaped the ferule to come under the fescue of an imprimatur? if serious and elaborate writings, as if they were no more than the theme of a grammar lad under his pedagogue, must not be uttered without the cursory eyes of a temporizing and extemporizing licenser? He who is not trusted with his own actions, his drift not being known to be evil, and standing to the hazard of law and penalty, has no great argument to think himself reputed in the Commonwealth wherein he was born for other than a fool or a foreigner. When a man writes to the world, he summons up all his reason and deliberation to assist him; he searches, meditates, is industrious, and likely consults and confers with his judicious friends; after all which done he takes himself to be informed in what he writes as well as any that wrote before him; if in this the most consummate act of his fidelity and ripeness, no years, no industry, no former proof of his abilities can bring him to that state of maturity as not to be still mistrusted and suspected, unless he carry all his considerate diligence, all his midnight watchings, and expense of Palladian oil, to the hasty view of an unleisured licenser, perhaps much his younger, perhaps far his inferior in judgment, perhaps one who never knew the labour of book-writing, and if he be not repulsed or slighted, must appear in print like a puny with his guardian and his censor's hand on the back of his title to be his bail and surety that he is no idiot or seducer, it cannot be but a dishonour and derogation to the author, to the book, to the privilege and dignity of learning. And what if the author shall be one so copious of fancy as to have many things well worth the adding come into his mind after licensing, while the book is yet under the press, which not seldom happens to the best and diligentest writers; and that perhaps a dozen times in one book? The printer dares not go beyond his licensed copy; so often then must the author trudge to his leave-giver, that those his new insertions may be viewed, and many a jaunt will be made ere that licenser, for it must be the same man, can either be found, or found at leisure; meanwhile either the press must stand still, which is no small damage, or the author lose his accuratest thoughts and send the book forth worse than he had made it, which to a diligent writer is the greatest melancholy and vexation that can befall. And how can a man teach with authority, which is the life of teaching, how can he be a doctor in his book as he ought to be, or else had better be silent, when as all he teaches, all he delivers, is but under the tuition, under the correction of his patriarchal licenser to blot or alter what precisely accords not with the hidebound humour which he calls his judgment; when every acute reader upon the first sight of a pedantic licence, will be ready with these like words to ding the book a quoit's distance from him :—" I hate a pupil teacher, I endure not an instructor that comes to me under the wardship of an overseeing fist; I know nothing of the licenser, but that I have his own hand here for his arrogance;

who shall warrant me his judgment?" "The State, sir," replies the stationer; but has a quick return, " The State shall be my governors, but not my critics; they may be mistaken in the choice of a licenser as easily as this licenser may be mistaken in an author: this is some common stuff;" and he might add from Sir Francis Bacon, that such authorized books are but the language of the times. For though a licenser should happen to be judicious more than ordinary, which will be a great jeopardy of the next succession, yet his very office and his commission enjoins him to let pass nothing but what is vulgarly received already. Nay, which is more lamentable, if the work of any deceased author, though never so famous in his lifetime and even to this day, come to their hands for licence to be printed or reprinted, if there be found in his book one sentence of a venturous edge, uttered in the height of zeal, and who knows whether it might not be the dictate of a divine spirit, yet not suiting with every low decrepit humour of their own, though it were Knox himself, the reformer of a kingdom, that spake it, they will not pardon him their dash; the sense of that great man shall to all posterity be lost for the fearfulness or the presumptuous rashness of a perfunctory licenser. And to what an author this violence hath been lately done, and in what book of greatest consequence to be faithfully published, I could now instance, but shall forbear till a more convenient season. Yet if these things be not resented seriously and timely by them who have the remedy in their power, but that such iron moulds as these shall have authority to gnaw out the choicest periods of exquisitest books, and to commit such a treacherous fraud against the orphan remainders of worthiest men after death, the more sorrow will belong to that hapless race of men whose misfortune it is to have understanding. Henceforth let no man care to learn, or care to be more than worldly wise; for certainly in higher matters to be ignorant and slothful, to be a common steadfast dunce, will be the only pleasant life and only in request.

And as it is a particular disesteem of every knowing person alive, and most injurious to the written labours and monuments of the dead, so to me it seems an undervaluing and vilifying of the whole nation. I cannot set so light by all the invention, the art, the wit, the grave and solid judgment which is in England, as that it can be comprehended in any twenty capacities how good soever; much less that it should not pass except their superintendence be over it, except it be sifted and strained with their strainers, that it should be uncurrent without their manual stamp. Truth and understanding are not such wares as to be monopolized and traded in by tickets and statutes and standards. We must not think to make a staple commodity of all the knowledge in the land, to mark and licence it like our broadcloth and our woolpacks. What is it but a servitude like that imposed by the Philistines, not to be allowed the sharpening of our own axes and coulters, but we must repair from all quarters to twenty licensing forges. Had any one written and divulged erroneous things and scandalous to honest life, misusing and forfeiting the esteem had of his reason among men, if after conviction this only censure were adjudged him, that he should never henceforth write but what were first examined by an appointed officer, whose hand should be annexed to pass his credit for him that now he might be safely read, it could not be apprehended less than a disgraceful punishment. Whence to include the whole nation, and those that never yet thus offended, under such a diffident and suspectful prohibition, may plainly be understood what a disparagement it is; so much the more, when as debtors and delinquents may walk abroad without a keeper, but inoffensive books must not stir forth without a visible gaoler in their title. Nor is it to the common people less than a reproach; for if we be so jealous over them as that we dare not trust them with an English pamphlet, what do we but censure them for a giddy, vicious, and ungrounded people, in such a sick and weak estate of faith and discretion as to be able to take nothing down but through the pipe of a licenser? That this is care or love of them we cannot pretend, when as in those Popish places where the laity are most hated and despised, the same strictness is used over them. Wisdom we cannot call it, because it stops but one breach of licence, nor that neither, when as those corruptions which it seeks to prevent break in faster at other doors which cannot be shut.

And in conclusion it reflects to the disrepute of our Ministers also, of whose labours we should hope better, and of the proficiency which their flock reaps by them, than that after all this light of the gospel which is, and is to be, and all this continual preaching, they should be still frequented with such an unprincipled, unedified, and laic rabble, as that the whiff of every new pamphlet should stagger them out of their catechism and Christian walking. This may have much reason to discourage the Ministers when such a low conceit is had of all their exhortations and the benefiting of their hearers, as that they are not thought fit to be turned loose to three sheets of paper without a licenser; that all the sermons, all the lectures preached, printed, vented in such numbers and such volumes as have now well-nigh made all other books unsaleable, should not be armour enough against one single enchiridion, without the Castle St. Angelo of an imprimatur.

And lest some should persuade ye, Lords and Commons, that these arguments of learned men's discouragement at this your order are mere flourishes and not real, I could recount what I have seen and heard in other countries, where this kind of inquisition tyrannizes; when I have sat among their learned men, for that honour I had, and been counted happy to be born in such a place of philosophic freedom as they supposed England was, while themselves did nothing but bemoan the servile condition into which learning amongst them was brought; that this was it which had damped the glory of Italian wits, that nothing had been there written now these many years but flattery and fustian. There it was that I found and visited the famous Galileo, grown old, a prisoner to the Inquisition for thinking in astronomy otherwise than the Franciscan and Dominican licensers thought. And though I knew that England then was groaning loudest under the prelatical yoke, nevertheless I took it as a pledge of future happiness that other nations were so persuaded of her liberty. Yet was it beyond my hope that those worthies were then breathing in her air who should be her leaders to such a deliverance as shall never be forgotten by any revolution of time that this world hath to finish. When that was once begun, it was as little in my fear, that what words of complaint I heard among learned men of other parts uttered against the Inquisition, the same I should hear by as learned men at home uttered in time of Parliament against an order of licensing; and that so generally, that when I disclosed myself a companion of their discontent, I might say, if without envy, that he whom an honest quæstorship had endeared to the Sicilians was not more by them importuned against Verres than the favourable opinion which I had among many who honour ye and are known and respected by ye, loaded me with entreaties and persuasions, that I would not despair to lay together that which just reason should bring into my mind toward the removal of an undeserved thraldom upon learning. That this is not, therefore, the disburdening of a particular fancy, but the common grievance of all those who had prepared their minds and studies above the vulgar pitch, to advance truth in others and from others to entertain it, thus much may satisfy. And in their name I shall for neither friend nor foe conceal what the general murmur is; that if it come to inquisitioning again and licensing, and that we are so timorous of ourselves, and so suspicious of all men, as to fear each book, and the shaking of every leaf, before we know what the contents are, if some who but of late were little better than silenced from preaching, shall come now to silence us from reading except what they please, it cannot be guessed what is intended by some but a second tyranny over learning; and will soon put it out of controversy that Bishops and Presbyters are the same to us, both name and thing. That those evils of Prelacy, which before from five or six and twenty Sees were distributively charged upon the whole people, will now light wholly upon learning, is not obscure to us: when as now the pastor of a small unlearned parish on the sudden shall be exalted Archbishop over a large diocese of books, and yet not remove, but keep his other cure too, a mystical pluralist. He who but of late cried down the sole ordination of every novice bachelor of art, and denied sole jurisdiction over the simplest parishioner, shall now, at home in his private chair, assume both these over worthiest and excellentest books and ablest authors that write them. This is not the covenants and protestations that we have made, this is not to put down Prelacy: this is but to chop an Episcopacy; this is but to translate the palace metropolitan from one kind of dominion into another; this is but an old canonical sleight of commuting our penance. To startle thus betimes at a mere unlicensed pamphlet will after a while be afraid of every conventicle, and a while after will make a conventicle of every Christian meeting. But I am certain that a State governed by the rules of justice and fortitude, or a Church built and founded upon the rock of faith and true knowledge, cannot be so pusillanimous. While things are yet not constituted in religion, that freedom of writing should be restrained by a discipline imitated from the Prelates and learned by them from the Inquisition, to shut us up all again into the breast of a licenser, must needs give cause of doubt and discouragement to all learned and religious men; who cannot but discern the fineness of this politic drift, and who are the contrivers: that while Bishops were to be baited down, then all presses might be open; it was the people's birthright and privilege in time of Parliament, it was the breaking forth of light. But now the Bishops abrogated and voided out of the Church, as if our reformation sought no more but to make room for others into their seats under another name, the Episcopal arts begin to bud again, the cruise of truth must run no more oil, liberty of printing must be enthralled again under a prelatical commission of twenty, the privilege of the people nullified, and which is worse, the freedom of learning must groan again and to her old fetters, all this the Parliament yet sitting. Although their own late arguments and defences against the Prelates might remember them that this obstructing violence meets for the most part with an event utterly opposite to the end which it drives at: instead of suppressing sects and schisms, it raises them and invests them with a reputation. "The punishing of wits enhances their authority," saith the Viscount St. Albans, "and a forbidden writing is thought to be a certain spark of truth that flies up in the faces of them who seek to tread it out." This order, therefore, may prove a nursing mother to sects, but I shall easily show how it will be a stepdame to truth: and first by disenabling us to the maintenance of what is known already.

Well knows he who uses to consider, that our faith and knowledge thrives by exercise as well as our limbs and complexion. Truth is compared in Scripture to a streaming fountain; if her waters flow not in a perpetual progression, they sicken into a muddy pool of conformity and tradition. A man may be a heretic in the truth; and if he believe things only because his pastor says so, or the assembly so determines, without knowing other reason, though his belief be true, yet the very truth he holds becomes his heresy. There is not any burden that some would gladlier post off to another than the charge and care of their religion. There be, who knows not that there be, of Protestants and professors who live and die in as arrant an implicit faith as any lay Papist of Loretto. A wealthy man, addicted to his pleasure and to his profits, finds religion to be a traffic so entangled, and of so many peddling accounts, that of all mysteries he cannot skill to keep a stock going upon that trade. What should he do? Fain he would have the name to be religious, fain he would bear up with his neighbours in that. What does he, therefore, but resolve to give over toiling, and to find himself out some factor to whose care and credit he may commit the whole managing of his religious affairs, some divine of note and estimation that must be. To him he adheres, resigns the whole warehouse of his religion, with all the locks and keys, into his custody; and indeed makes the very person of that man his religion, esteems his associating with him a sufficient evidence and commendatory of his own piety. So that a man may say his religion is now no more within himself, but is become a dividual movable, and goes and comes near him according as that good man frequents the house. He entertains him, gives him gifts, feasts him, lodges him; his religion comes home at night, prays, is liberally supped, and sumptuously laid to sleep; rises, is saluted, and after the malmsey, or some well-spiced brewage, and better breakfasted than he whose morning appetite would have gladly fed on green figs between Bethany and Jerusalem; his religion walks abroad at eight, and leaves his kind entertainer in the shop trading all day without his religion.

Another sort there be who when they hear that all things shall be ordered, all things regulated and settled, nothing written but what passes through the custom-house of certain publicans that have the tunaging and the poundaging of all free spoken truth, will straight give themselves up into your hands; make them and cut them out what religion ye please. There be delights, there be recreations and jolly pastimes that will fetch the day about from sun to sun, and rock the tedious year as in a delightful dream. What need they torture their heads with that which others have taken so strictly and so unalterably into their own purveying? These are the fruits which a dull ease and cessation of our knowledge will bring forth among the people. How goodly and how to be wished were such an obedient unanimity as this, what a fine conformity would it starch us all into? Doubtless a staunch and solid piece of framework as any January could freeze together.

Nor much better will be the consequence even among the clergy themselves. It is no new thing never heard of before for a parochial minister, who has his reward and is at his Hercules' Pillars in a warm benefice, to be easily inclinable, if he have nothing else that may rouse up his studies, to finish his circuit in an English concordance and a topic folio, the gatherings and savings of a sober graduate-ship, a harmony and a catena, treading the constant round of certain common doctrinal heads, attended with their uses, motives, marks and means, out of which as out of an alphabet or sol fa, by forming and transforming, joining and disjoining variously a little book-craft, and two hours' meditation might furnish him unspeakably to the performance of more than a weekly charge of sermoning, not to reckon up the infinite helps of interlinearies, breviaries, synopses, and other loitering gear. But as for the multitude of sermons ready printed and piled up, on every text that is not difficult, our London trading St. Thomas in his vestry, and add to boot St. Martin and St. Hugh, have not within their hallowed limits more vendible ware of all sorts ready made; so that penury he never need fear of pulpit provision, having where so plenteously to refresh his magazine. But if his rear and flanks be not impaled, if his back door be not secured by the rigid licenser, but that a bold book may now and then issue forth, and give the assault to some of his old collections in their trenches, it will concern him then to keep waking, to stand in watch, to set good guards and sentinels about his received opinions, to walk the round and counter-round with his fellow-inspectors, fearing lest any of his flock be seduced, who also then would be better instructed, better exercised and disciplined. And God send that the fear of this diligence which must then be used, do not make us affect the laziness of a licensing Church.

For if we be sure we are in the right, and do not hold the truth guiltily, which becomes not, if we ourselves condemn not our own weak and frivolous teaching, and the people for an untaught and irreligious gadding rout, what can be more fair than when a man judicious, learned, and of a conscience, for aught we know, as good as theirs that taught us what we know, shall not privily from house to house, which is more dangerous, but openly by writing publish to the world what his opinion is, what his reasons, and wherefore that which is now thought cannot be sound? Christ urged it as wherewith to justify himself, that He preached in public; yet writing is more public than preaching, and more easy to refutation, if need be, there being so many whose business and profession merely it is to be the champions of truth, which, if they neglect, what can be imputed but their sloth or inability?

Thus much we are hindered and disinured by this course of licensing towards the true knowledge of what we seem to know. For how much it hurts and hinders the licensers themselves in the calling of their ministry, more than any secular employment, if they will discharge that office as they ought, so that of necessity they must neglect either the one duty or the other, I insist not, because it is a particular, but leave it to their own conscience, how they will decide it there.

There is yet behind of what I purposed to lay open, the incredible loss and detriment that this plot of licensing puts us to. More than if some enemy at sea should stop up all our havens and ports and creeks, it hinders and retards the importation of our richest merchandise, truth; nay, it was first established and put in practice by antichristian malice and mystery on set purpose to extinguish, if it were possible, the light of Reformation, and to settle falsehood, little differing from that policy wherewith the Turk upholds his Alcoran by the prohibition of printing. It is not denied, but gladly confessed, we are to send our thanks and vows to heaven louder than most of nations for that great measure of truth which we enjoy, especially in those main points between us and the Pope with his appurtenances the prelates; but he who thinks we are to pitch our tent here, and have attained the utmost prospect of reformation that the mortal glass wherein we contemplate can show us, till we come to beatific vision, that man by this very opinion declares that he is yet far short of truth.

Truth indeed came once into the world with her Divine Master, and was a perfect shape most glorious to look on; but when He ascended, and his Apostles after Him were laid asleep, then straight arose a wicked race of deceivers, who, as that story goes of the Egyptian Typhon with his conspirators how they dealt with the good Osiris, took the virgin truth, hewed her lovely form into a thousand pieces, and scattered them to the four winds. From that time ever since, the sad friends of truth, such as dost appear, imitating the careful search that Isis made for the mangled body of Osiris, went up and down gathering up limb by limb still as they could find them. We have not yet found them all, Lords and Commons, nor ever shall do, till her Master's second coming; He shall bring together every joint and member, and shall mould them into an immortal feature of loveliness and perfection. Suffer not these licensing prohibitions to stand at every place of opportunity forbidding and disturbing them that continue seeking, that continue to do our obsequies to the torn body of our martyred saint. We boast our light; but if we look not wisely on the sun itself, it smites us into darkness. Who can discern those planets that are oft combust, and those stars of brightest magnitude that rise and set with the sun, until the opposite motion of their orbs bring them to such a place in the firmament, where they may be seen evening or morning? The light which we have gained was given us, not to be ever staring on, but by it to discover onward things more remote from our knowledge. It is not the unfrocking of a priest, the unmitring of a bishop, and the removing him from off the Presbyterian shoulders that will make us a happy nation; no, if other things as great in the Church and in the rule of life both economical and political be not looked into and reformed, we have looked so long upon the blaze that Zuinglius and Calvin hath beaconed up to us, that we are stark blind. There be who perpetually complain of schisms and sects, and make it such a calamity that any man dissents from their maxims. It is their own pride and ignorance which causes the disturbing, who neither will hear with meekness nor can convince; yet all must be suppressed which is not found in their syntagma. They are the troublers, they are the dividers of unity, who neglect and permit not others to unite those dissevered pieces which are yet wanting to the body of truth. To be still searching what we know not by what we know, still closing up truth to truth as we find it (for all her body is homogeneal and proportional), this is the golden rule in theology as well as in arithmetic, and makes up the best harmony in a Church, not the forced and outward union of cold and neutral and inwardly divided minds.

Lords and Commons of England, consider what nation it is whereof ye are and whereof ye are the governors: a nation not slow and dull, but of a quick, ingenious, and piercing spirit, acute to invent, subtle and sinewy to discourse, not beneath the reach of any point the highest that human capacity can soar to. Therefore the studies of learning in her deepest sciences have been so ancient and so eminent among us, that writers of good antiquity and ablest judgment have been persuaded that even the school of Pythagoras and the Persian wisdom took beginning from the old philosophy of this island. And that wise and civil Roman, Julius Agricola, who governed once here for Cæsar, preferred the natural wits of Britain before the laboured studies of the French. Nor is it for nothing that the grave and frugal Transylvanian sends out yearly from as far as the mountainous borders of Russia and beyond the Hercynian wilderness, not their youth, but their staid men, to learn our language and our theologic arts. Yet that which is above all this, the favour and the love of heaven, we have great argument to think in a peculiar manner propitious and propending towards us. Why else was this nation chosen before any other, that out of her as out of Sion should be proclaimed and sounded forth the first tidings and trumpet of Reformation to all Europe? And had it not been the obstinate perverseness of our prelates against the divine and admirable spirit of Wickliff, to suppress him as a schismatic and innovator, perhaps neither the Bohemian Huss and Jerome, no, nor the name of Luther or of Calvin, had been ever known; the glory of reforming all our neighbours had been completely ours. But now, as our obdurate clergy have with violence demeaned the matter, we are become hitherto the latest and the backwardest scholars, of whom God offered to have made us the teachers. Now once again, by all concurrence of signs and by the general instinct of holy and devout men, as they daily and solemnly express their thoughts, God is decreeing to begin some new and great period in his Church, even to the reforming of Reformation itself. What does He then but reveal himself to his servants, and as his manner is, first to his Englishmen: I say as his manner is, first to us, though we mark not the method of his counsels and are unworthy? Behold now this vast city: a city of refuge, the mansion house of liberty, encompassed and surrounded with his protection; the shop of war hath not there more anvils and hammers waking, to fashion out the plates and instruments of armed justice in defence of beleaguered truth, than there be pens and heads there, sitting by their studious lamps, musing, searching, revolving new notions and ideas wherewith to present as with their homage and their fealty the approaching Reformation, others as fast reading, trying all things, assenting to the force of reason and convincement. What could a man require more from a nation so pliant and so prone to seek after knowledge? What wants there to such a towardly and pregnant soil but wise and faithful labourers, to make a knowing people, a nation of prophets, of sages, and of worthies? We reckon more than five months yet to harvest; there need not be five weeks; had we but eyes to lift up, the fields are white already. Where there is much desire to learn, there of necessity will be much arguing, much writing, many opinions; for opinion in good men is but knowledge in the making. Under these fantastic terrors of sect and schism, we wrong the earnest and zealous thirst after knowledge and understanding which God hath stirred up in this city. What some lament of, we rather should rejoice at, should rather praise this pious forwardness among men to reassume the ill deputed care of their religion into their own hands again. A little generous prudence, a little forbearance of one another and some grain of charity, might win all these diligences to join and unite in one general and brotherly search after truth, could we but forego this prelatical tradition of crowding free consciences and Christian liberties into canons and precepts of men. I doubt not, if some great and worthy stranger should come among us, wise to discern the mould and temper of a people and how to govern it, observing the high hopes and aims, the diligent alacrity of our extended thoughts and reasonings in the pursuance of truth and freedom, but that he would cry out as Pyrrhus did, admiring the Roman docility and courage: "If such were my Epirots, I would not despair the greatest design that could be attempted to make a church or kingdom happy." Yet these are the men cried out against for schismatics and sectaries; as if, while the Temple of the Lord was building, some cutting, some squaring the marble, others hewing the cedars, there should be a sort of irrational men who could not consider there must be many schisms and many dissections made in the quarry and in the timber, ere the house of God can be built. And when every stone is laid artfully together, it cannot be united into a continuity, it can but be contiguous in this world; neither can every piece of the building be of one form; nay, rather the perfection consists in this: that out of many moderate varieties and brotherly dissimilitudes that are not vastly disproportional arises the goodly and the graceful symmetry that commends the whole pile and structure. Let us therefore be more considerate builders, more wise in spiritual architecture, when great reformation is expected. For now the time seems come, wherein Moses the great Prophet may sit in heaven rejoicing to see that memorable and glorious wish of his fulfilled, when not only our seventy elders but all the Lord's people are become prophets. No marvel then, though some men, and some good men too perhaps, but young in goodness, as Joshua then was, envy them. They fret, and out of their own weakness are in agony, lest those divisions and subdivisions will undo us. The adversary again applauds, and waits the hour; when they have branched themselves out, saith he, small enough into parties and partitions, then will be our time. Fool! he sees not the firm root, out of which we all grow though into branches; nor will beware until he see our small divided maniples cutting through at every angle of his ill-united and unwieldy brigade. And that we are to hope better of all these supposed sects and schisms, and that we shall not need that solicitude, honest perhaps, though over-timorous of them that vex in this behalf, but shall laugh in the end at those malicious applauders of our differences, I have these reasons to persuade me:

First, when a city shall be as it were besieged and blocked about, her navigable river infested, inroads and incursions round, defiance and battle oft rumoured to be marching up even to her walls and suburb trenches, that then the people, or the greater part, more than at other times, wholly taken up with the study of highest and most important matters to be reformed, should be disputing, reasoning, reading, inventing, discoursing, even to a rarity and admiration, things not before discoursed or written of, argues first a singular goodwill, contentedness and confidence in your prudent foresight and safe government, Lords and Commons; and from thence derives itself to a gallant bravery and well-grounded contempt of their enemies, as if there were no small number of as great spirits among us, as his was, who when Rome was nigh besieged by Hannibal, being in the city, bought that piece of ground at no cheap rate whereon Hannibal himself encamped his own regiment. Next, it is a lively and cheerful presage of our happy success and victory. For as in a body, when the blood is fresh, the spirits pure and vigorous, not only to vital but to rational faculties, and those in the acutest and the pertest operations of wit and subtlety, it argues in what good plight and constitution the body is, so when the cheerfulness of the people is so sprightly up, as that it has not only wherewith to guard well its own freedom and safety but to spare, and to bestow upon the solidest and sublimest points of controversy and new invention, it betokens us not degenerated, nor drooping to a fatal decay, but casting off the old and wrinkled skin of corruption to outlive these pangs and wax young again, entering the glorious ways of truth and prosperous virtue, destined to become great and honourable in these latter ages. Methinks I see in my mind a noble and puissant nation rousing herself like a strong man after sleep, and shaking her invincible locks. Methinks I see her as an eagle mewing her mighty youth, and kindling her undazzled eyes at the full mid-day beam, purging and unscaling her long abused sight at the fountain itself of heavenly radiance, while the whole noise of timorous and flocking birds, with those also that love the twilight, flutter about, amazed at what she means, and in their envious gabble would prognosticate a year of sects and schisms.

What should ye do then, should ye suppress all this flowery crop of knowledge and new light sprung up and yet springing daily in this city, should ye set an oligarchy of twenty ingrossers over it, to bring a famine upon our minds again, when we shall know nothing but what is measured to us by their bushel? Believe it, Lords and Commons, they who counsel ye to such a suppressing do as good as bid ye suppress yourselves; and I will soon show how. If it be desired to know the immediate cause of all this free writing and free speaking, there cannot be assigned a truer than your own mild and free and human government; it is the liberty, Lords and Commons, which your own valorous and happy counsels have purchased us, liberty which is the nurse of all great wits; this is that which hath rarefied and enlightened our spirits like the influence of heaven; this is that which hath enfranchised, enlarged and lifted up our apprehensions degrees above themselves. Ye cannot make us now less capable, less knowing, less eagerly pursuing of the truth, unless ye first make yourselves, that made us so, less the lovers, less the founders of our true liberty. We can grow ignorant again, brutish, formal, and slavish, as ye found us; but you then must first become that which ye cannot be, oppressive, arbitrary, and tyrannous, as they were from whom ye have freed us. That our hearts are now more capacious, our thoughts more erected to the search and expectation of greatest and exactest things, is the issue of your own virtue propagated in us; ye cannot suppress that unless ye reinforce an abrogated and merciless law, that fathers may dispatch at will their own children. And who shall then stick closest to ye, and excite others? Not he who takes up arms for cote and conduct and his four nobles of Danegelt. Although I dispraise not the defence of just immunities, yet love my peace better, if that were all. Give me the liberty to know, to utter, and to argue freely according to conscience, above all liberties.

What would be best advised then, if it be found so hurtful and so unequal to suppress opinions for the newness or the unsuitableness to a customary acceptance, will not be my task to say; I only shall repeat what I have learnt from one of your own honourable number, a right noble and pious lord, who had he not sacrificed his life and fortunes to the Church and Commonwealth, we had not now missed and bewailed a worthy and undoubted patron of this argument. Ye know him I am sure; yet I for honour's sake, and may it be eternal to him, shall name him, the Lord Brook. He writing of Episcopacy, and by the way treating of sects and schisms, left ye his vote, or rather now the last words of his dying charge, which I know will ever be of dear and honoured regard with ye, so full of meekness and breathing charity, that next to his last testament, who bequeathed love and peace to his disciples, I cannot call to mind where I have read or heard words more mild and peaceful. He there exhorts us to hear with patience and humility those, however they be miscalled, that desire to live purely, in such a use of God's Ordinances, as the best guidance of their conscience gives them, and to tolerate them, though in some disconformity to ourselves. The book itself will tell us more at large, being published to the world and dedicated to the Parliament by him who both for his life and for his death deserves that what advice he left be not laid by without perusal.

And now the time in special is by privilege to write and speak what may help to the further discussing of matters in agitation. The Temple of

Janus with his two controversal faces might now not insignificantly be set open. And though all the winds of doctrine were let loose to play upon the earth, so truth be in the field, we do injuriously by licensing and prohibiting to misdoubt her strength. Let her and falsehood grapple ; who ever knew truth put to the worse in a free and open encounter ? Her confuting is the best and surest suppressing. He who hears what praying there is for light and clearer knowledge to be sent down among us, would think of other matters to be constituted beyond the discipline of Geneva, framed and fabricked already to our hands. Yet when the new light which we beg for shines in upon us, there be who envy and oppose if it come not first in at their casements. What a collusion is this, when as we are exhorted by the wise man to use diligence, to seek for wisdom as for hidden treasures early and late, that another order shall enjoin us to know nothing but by statute! When a man hath been labouring the hardest labour in the deep mines of knowledge, hath furnished out his findings in all their equipage, drawn forth his reasons as it were a battle ranged, scattered and defeated all objections in his way, calls out his adversary into the plain, offers him the advantage of wind and sun, if he please, only that he may try the matter by dint of argument, for his opponents then to skulk, to lay ambushments, to keep a narrow bridge of licensing where the challenger should pass, though it be valour enough in soldiership, is but weakness and cowardice in the wars of truth. For who knows not that truth is strong next to the Almighty? She needs no policies, no stratagems, nor licensings to make her victorious; those are the shifts and the defences that error uses against her power. Give her but room, and do not bind her when she sleeps, for then she speaks not true, as the old Proteus did, who spake oracles only when he was caught and bound; but then rather she turns herself into all shapes except her own, and perhaps tunes her voice according to the time, as Micaiah did before Ahab, until she be adjured into her own likeness. Yet is it not impossible that she may have more shapes than one. What else is all that rank of things indifferent, wherein truth may be on this side or on the other without being unlike herself? What but a vain shadow else is the abolition of those Ordinances, that handwriting nailed to the cross, what great purchase is this Christian liberty which Paul so often boasts of? His doctrine is, that he who eats or eats not, regards a day or regards it not, may do either to the Lord. How many other things might be tolerated in peace and left to conscience, had we but charity, and were it not the chief stronghold of our hypocrisy to be ever judging one another. I fear yet this iron yoke of outward conformity hath left a slavish print upon our necks; the ghost of a linen decency yet haunts us. We stumble and are impatient at the least dividing of one visible congregation from another, though it be not in fundamentals; and through our forwardness to suppress, and our backwardness to recover any enthralled piece of truth out of the grip of custom, we care not to keep truth separated from truth, which is the fiercest rent and disunion of all. We do not see that, while we still affect by all means a rigid external formality, we may as soon fall again into a gross conforming stupidity, a stark and dead congealment of wood and hay and stubble forced and frozen together, which is more to the sudden degenerating of a Church than many subdichotomies of petty schisms. Not that I can think well of every light separation, or that all in a Church is to be expected gold and silver and precious stones; it is not possible for man to sever the wheat from the tares, the good fish from the other fry; that must be the angels' ministry at the end of mortal things. Yet if all cannot be of one mind—as who looks they should be?—this doubtless is more wholesome, more prudent, and more Christian: that many be tolerated rather than all compelled. I mean not tolerated Popery and open superstition, which as it extirpates all religions and civil supremacies, so itself should be extirpated, provided first that all charitable and compassionate means be used to win and regain the weak and misled; that also which is impious or evil absolutely either against faith or manners no law can possibly permit, that intends not to unlaw itself; but those neighbouring differences, or rather indifferences, are what I speak of, whether in some point of doctrine or of discipline, which though they may be many, yet need not interrupt the unity of spirit, if we could but find among us the bond of peace. In the meanwhile if any one would write, and bring his helpful hand to the slow-moving reformation which we labour under, if truth have spoken to him before others, or but seemed at least to speak, who hath so bejesuited us that we should trouble that man with asking licence to do so worthy a deed? And not consider this, that if it come to prohibiting, there is not aught more likely to be prohibited than truth itself; whose first appearance to our eyes, bleared and dimmed with prejudice and custom, is more unsightly and unplausible than many errors, even as the person is of many a great man slight and comtemptible to see to. And what do they tell us vainly of new opinions, when this very opinion of theirs, that none must be heard but whom they like, is the worst and newest opinion of all others; and is the chief cause why sects and schisms do so much abound, and true knowledge is kept at distance from us? Besides yet a greater danger which is in it: for when God shakes a kingdom with strong and healthful commotions to a general reforming, it is not untrue that many sectaries and false teachers are then busiest in seducing; but yet more true it is, that God then raises to his own work men of rare abilities and more than common industry, not only to look back and revise what hath been taught heretofore, but to gain further and go on some new enlightened steps in the discovery of truth. For such is the order of God's enlightening his Church, to dispense and deal out by degrees his beam, so as our earthly eyes may best sustain it. Neither is God appointed and confined, where and out of what place these his chosen shall be first heard to speak; for He sees not as man sees, chooses not as man chooses, lest we should devote ourselves again to set places and assemblies and outward callings of men, planting our faith one while in the old Convocation house and another while in the chapel at Westminster; when all the faith and religion that shall be there canonized is not sufficient, without plain convincement and the charity of patient instruction, to supple the least bruise of conscience, to edify the meanest Christian, who desires to walk in the spirit and not in the letter of human trust, for all the number of voices that can be there made; no, though Harry the Seventh himself there, with all his liege tombs about him, should lend them voices from the dead to swell their number. And if the men be erroneous who appear to be the leading schismatics, what withholds us but our sloth, our self-will, and distrust in the right cause, that we do not give them gentle meetings and gentle dismissions, that we debate not and examine the matter thoroughly with liberal and frequent audience; if not for their sakes, yet for our own, seeing no man who hath tasted learning but will confess the many ways of profiting by those who, not contented with stale receipts, are able to manage and set forth new positions to the world? And were they but as the dust and cinders of our feet, so long as in that notion they may serve to polish and brighten the armoury of truth, even for that respect they were not utterly to be cast away. But if they be of those whom God hath fitted for the special use of these times with eminent and ample gifts, and those, perhaps, neither among the priests nor among the Pharisees, and we, in the haste of a precipitant zeal, shall make no distinction, but resolve to stop their mouths, because we fear they come with new and dangerous opinions, as we commonly forejudge them ere we understand them, no less then woe to us, while, thinking thus to defend the Gospel, we are found the persecutors.

There have been not a few since the beginning of this Parliament, both of the Presbytery and others, who by their unlicensed books to the contempt of an imprimatur first broke that triple ice clung about our hearts, and taught the people to see day. I hope that none of those were the persuaders to renew upon us this bondage which they themselves have wrought so much good by contemning. But if neither the check that Moses gave to young Joshua, nor the countermand which our Saviour gave to young John, who was so ready to prohibit those whom he thought unlicensed, be not enough to admonish our elders how unacceptable to God their testy mood of prohibiting is, if neither their own remembrance what evil hath abounded in the Church by this let of licensing, and what good they themselves have begun by transgressing it, be not enough, but that they will persuade and execute the most Dominican part of the Inquisition over us, and are already with one foot in the stirrup so active at suppressing, it would be no unequal distribution in the first place to suppress the suppressors themselves, whom the change of their condition hath puffed up more than their late experience of harder times hath made wise.

And as for regulating the Press, let no man think to have the honour of advising ye better than yourselves have done in that order published next before this: that no book be printed, unless the printer's, and the author's name, or at least the printer's be registered. Those which otherwise come forth, if they be found mischievous and libellous, the fire and the executioner will be the timeliest and the most effectual remedy that man's prevention can use. For this authentic Spanish policy of licensing books, if I have said aught, will prove the most unlicensed book itself within a short while; and was the immediate image of a Star Chamber decree to that purpose made in those very times when that Court did the rest of those her pious works, for which she is now fallen from the stars with Lucifer. Whereby ye may guess what kind of State prudence, what love of the people, what care of religion or good manners there was at the contriving, although with singular hypocrisy it pretended to bind books to their good behaviour. And how it got the upper hand of your precedent order so well constituted before, if we may believe those men whose profession gives them cause to inquire most, it may be doubted there was in it the fraud of some old patentees and monopolizers in the trade of book selling, who, under pretence of the poor in their company not to be defrauded, and the just retaining of each man his several copy, which God forbid should be gainsaid, brought divers glozing colours to the House, which were indeed but colours, and serving to no end except it be to exercise a superiority over their neighbours, men who do not therefore labour in an honest profession to which learning is indebted, that they should be made other men's vassals. Another end is thought was aimed at by some of them in procuring by petition this order, that having power in their hands, malignant books might the easier escape abroad, as the event shows. But of these sophisms and elenchs of merchandise I skill not. This I know, that errors in a good government and in a bad are equally almost incident; for what magistrate may not be misinformed, and much the sooner, if liberty of printing be reduced into the power of a few? But to redress willingly and speedily what hath been erred, and in highest authority to esteem a plain advertisement more than others have done a sumptuous bribe, is a virtue (honoured Lords and Commons) answerable to your highest actions, and whereof none can participate but greatest and wisest men.

KILLING NO MURDER,

BRIEFLY DISCOURSED, IN

THREE QUESTIONS, FIT FOR PUBLIC VIEW,

TO DETER AND PREVENT

TYRANTS FROM USURPING SUPREME POWER.

And all the people of the land rejoiced; and the city was quiet, after that they had slain Athaliah with the sword.—2 CHRON. xxiii. 21.

Now after the time that Amaziah did turn away from following the Lord, they made a conspiracy against him in Jerusalem, and he fled to Lachish; but they sent to Lachish after him, and slew him there.—2 CHRON. xxv. 27.

TO

HIS HIGHNESS OLIVER CROMWELL.

MAY IT PLEASE YOUR HIGHNESS,

How I have spent some hours of the leisure your Highness hath been pleased to give me this following paper will give your Highness an account. How you will please to interpret it I cannot tell; but I can with confidence say, my intention in it is to procure your Highness that justice nobody yet does you, and to let the people see the longer they defer it the greater injury they do both themselves and you. To your Highness justly belongs the honour of dying for the people; and it cannot choose but be unspeakable consolation to you in the last moments of your life to consider with how much benefit to the world you are like to leave it. It is then only, my Lord, the titles you now usurp will be truly yours; you will then be indeed the deliverer of your country, and free it from a bondage little inferior to that from which Moses delivered his.

You will then be that true reformer which you would be thought. Religion shall be then restored, liberty asserted, and Parliaments have those privileges they have fought for. We shall then hope that other laws will have place besides those of the sword, and that justice shall be otherwise defined than the will and pleasure of the strongest; and we shall then hope men will keep oaths again, and not have the necessity of being false and perfidious to preserve themselves, and be like their rulers. All this we hope from your Highness's happy expiration, who are the true father of your country; for while you live we can call nothing ours, and it is from your death that we hope for our inheritances. Let this consideration arm and fortify your Highness's mind against the fears of death, and the terrors of your evil conscience, that the good you will do by your death will something balance the evils of your life. And if in the black catalogue of high malefactor few can be found that have lived more to the affliction and disturbance of mankind than your Highness hath done, yet your greatest enemies will not deny but there are likewise as few that have expired more to the universal benefit of mankind than your Highness is like to do. To hasten this great good is the chief end of my writing this paper; and if it have the effects I hope it will, your Highness will quickly be out of the reach of men's malice, and your enemies will only be able to wound you in your memory, which strokes you will not feel. That your Highness may be speedily in this security is the universal wishes of your grateful country. This is the desires and prayers of the good and of the bad, and it may be is the only thing wherein all sects and factions do agree in their devotions, and is our only common prayer. But amongst all that put in their requests and supplications for your Highness's speedy deliverances from all earthly troubles, none is more assiduous nor more fervent than he who, with the rest of the nation, hath the honour to be,

  May it please your Highness,
  Your Highness's present slave and vassal,
        W. A.

KILLING NO MURDER.

IT is not any ambition to be in print, when so few spare paper and the press, nor any instigations of private revenge or malice (though few that dare be honest now want their causes), that have prevailed with me to make myself the author of a pamphlet, and to disturb that quiet which at present I enjoy by his Highness's great favour and injustice. Nor am I ignorant to how little purpose I shall employ that time and pains which I shall bestow upon this paper. For to think that any reasons or persuasions of mine, or conviction of their own, shall draw men from any thing wherein they see profit or security, or to any thing wherein they fear loss or see danger, is to have a better opinion both of myself and them than either of us both deserve.

Besides, the subject itself is of that nature, that I am not only to expect danger from ill men, but censure and disallowance from many that are good; for these opinions only looked upon, not looked into (which all have not eyes for), will appear bloody and cruel; and these compellations I must expect from those that have a zeal, but not according to knowledge; if, therefore, I had considered myself, I had spared whatever this is of pains, and not distasted so many, to please so few as are in mankind the honest and the wise. But at such a time as this, when God is not only exercising us with a usual and common calamity, of letting us fall into slavery that used our liberty so ill, but is pleased so far to bind our understandings and to debase our spirits as to suffer us to court our bondage, and to place it amongst the requests we put up to Him, indignation makes a man break that silence that prudence would persuade him to use, if not to work upon other men's minds, yet to ease his own.

A late pamphlet tells us of a great design discovered against the person of his Highness, and of the Parliament's coming (for so does that Junto profane that name) to congratulate with his Highness his happy deliverance from that wicked and bloody attempt. Besides this, that they have ordered that God Almighty shall be mocked with a day of thanksgiving (as I think, the world is with the plot), and that the people shall give public thanks for the public calamity that God is yet pleased to continue his judgments upon them and to frustrate all means that are used for their deliverance. Certainly none will now deny that the English are a very thankful people. But I think if we had read in Scripture that the Israelites had cried unto the Lord, not for their own deliverance, but the preservation of their task-masters, and that they had thanked God with solemnity that Pharaoh was yet living, and that there was still great hopes of the daily increase of the number of their bricks: though that people did so many things not only impiously and profanely but ridiculously and absurdly, yet certainly they did nothing we should more have wondered at than to have found them ceremoniously thankful to God for plagues, that were commonly so brutishly unthankful for mercies; and we should have thought that Moses had done them a great deal of wrong if he had not suffered them to enjoy their slavery, and left them to their tasks and garlic.

I can with justice say, my principal intention in this paper is not to declaim against my Lord Protector or his accomplices; for, were it not more to justify others than to accuse them, I should think their own actions did that work sufficiently, and I should not take pains to tell the world what they knew before. My design is, to examine whether if there hath been such a plot as we hear of, and that it was contrived by Mr. Sindercombe against my Lord Protector, and not by my Lord Protector against Mr. Sindercombe (which is doubtful); whether it deserves those epithets Mr. Speaker is pleased to give it, of bloody, wicked, and proceeding from the Prince of Darkness. I know very well how incapable the vulgar are of considering what is extraordinary and singular in every case, and that they judge of things and name them by their exterior appearances, without penetrating at all into their causes or natures. And without doubt, when they hear the Protector was to be killed, they straight conclude a man was to be murdered, not a malefactor punished; for they think the formalities do always make the things themselves, and that it is the judge and the crier that makes the justice, and the gaol the criminal; and therefore when they read in the pamphlet Mr. Speaker's speech, they certainly think he gives these plotters their right titles, and, as readily as a High Court of Justice, they condemn them, without ever examining whether they would have killed a magistrate or destroyed a tyrant over whom every man is naturally a judge and an executioner, and whom the laws of God, of Nature, and of nations expose like beasts of prey to be destroyed as they are met.

That I may be as plain as I can, I shall first make it a question—which indeed is none— whether my Lord Protector be a tyrant or not? Secondly, if he be, whether it is lawful to do justice upon him without solemnity, that is, to kill him? Thirdly, if it be lawful, whether it is like to prove profitable or noxious to the Commonwealth?

The civil law makes tyrants of two sorts, "tyrannus sine titulo" and "tyrannus exercitio." The one is called a tyrant because he hath no right to govern; the other because he governs tyrannically. We will very briefly discourse of them both, and see whether the Protector may not with great justice put in his claim to both titles.

We shall sufficiently demonstrate who they are that have not a right to govern, if we show who they are that have; and what it is that makes the power just which those that rule have over the natural liberty of other men. To fathers, within their private families, Nature hath given a supreme power. Every man, says Aristotle, of right governs his wife and children, and this power was necessarily exercised everywhere, whilst families lived dispersed, before the constitutions of Commonwealths; and in many places it continued after, as appears by the laws of Solon and the most ancient of those of Rome. And indeed, as by the laws of God and Nature, the care, defence, and support of the family lies upon every man whose it is, so by the same law there is due unto every man from his family a subjection and obedience in compensation of that support. But several families uniting themselves together to make up one body of a Commonwealth, and being independent one of another, without any natural superiority or obligation, nothing can introduce amongst them a disparity of rule and subjection but some power that is over them, which power none can pretend to have but God and themselves.

Wherefore all power which is lawfully exercised over such a society of men (which from the end of its institution we call a Commonwealth) must necessarily be derived, either from the appointment of God Almighty, who is Supreme Lord of all and every part, or from the consent of the society itself, who have the next power to his of disposing of their own liberty as they shall think fit for their own good. This power God hath given to societies of men, as well as He gave it to particular persons; and when He interposes not his own authority, and appoints not himself who shall be his vicegerents and rule under Him, He leaves it to none but the people themselves to make the election, whose benefit is the end of all government. Nay, when He himself hath been pleased to appoint rulers for that people which He was pleased peculiarly to own, He many times made the choice, but left the confirmation and ratification of that choice to the people themselves. So Saul was chosen by God, and anointed king by his prophet, but made king by all the people at Gilgal. David was anointed king by the same prophet, but was afterwards, after Saul's death, confirmed by the people of Judah, and seven years after by the elders of Israel, the people's deputies at Chebron. And it is observable, that though they knew that David was appointed king by God, and anointed by his prophet, yet they likewise knew that God allowed to themselves not only his confirmation, but likewise the limitation of his power; for before his inauguration they made a league with him—that is, obliged him by compact to the performance of such conditions as they thought necessary for the securing their liberty. Nor is it less remarkable that, when God gives directions to his people concerning their government, He plainly leaves the form to themselves: for He says not, When thou shalt have come into the land which the Lord thy God gives thee, "statues super te regem," but "Si dixeris statuam." God says not, Thou shalt appoint a king over thee; but if thou shalt say, I will appoint; leaving it to their choice whether they would say so or no. And it is plain in that place that God gives the people the choice of their king, for He there instructs them whom they shall choose, "E medio fratrum tuorum," one out of the midst of thy brethren. Much more might we say, if it were a less manifest truth that all just power of government is founded upon these two bases, of God's immediate command, or the people's consent; and, therefore, whosoever arrogates to himself that power, or any part of it, that cannot produce one of those two titles, is not a ruler, but an invader, and those that are subject to that power are not governed, but oppressed.

This being considered, have not the people of England much reason to ask the Protector this question, "Quis constituit te virum principem et judicem super nos?" Who made thee a prince and a judge over us? If God made thee, make it manifest to us. If the people, where did we meet to do it? Who took our subscriptions? To whom deputed we our authority? And when and where did those deputies make the choice? Sure these interrogations are very natural, and I believe would much trouble his Highness's Council and his Junto to answer. In a word, that I may not tire my reader, who will not want proofs for what I say, if he wants not memory: if to change the Government without the people's consent; if to dissolve their representatives by force, and disannul their acts; if to give the name of the people's representatives to confederates of his own, that he may establish iniquity by a law; if to take away men's lives out of all course of law, by certain murderers of his own appointment, whom he names a High Court of Justice; if to decimate men's estates, and by his own power to impose upon the people what taxes he pleases, and to maintain all by force of arms; if, I say, all this does make a tyrant, his own impudence cannot deny but he is as complete a one as ever hath been since there have been societies of men. He that hath done, and does all this, is the person for whose preservation the people of England must pray; but certainly if they do, it is for the same reason that the old woman of Syracuse prayed for the long life of the tyrant Dionysius, lest the devil should come next.

Now if, instead of God's command, or the people's

consent, his Highness hath no other title but force and fraud, which is to want all title; and if to violate all laws, and propose none to rule by but those of his own will, be to exercise that tyranny he hath usurped, and to make his administration conformable to his claim, then the first question we proposed is a question no longer.

But before we come to the second, being things are more easily perceived and found by the description of their exterior accidents and qualities than the defining their essences, it will not be amiss to see whether his Highness hath not as well the outward marks and characters by which tyrants are known, as he hath their nature and essential properties: whether he hath not the skin of the lion and tail of the fox, as well as he hath the violence of the one and deceit of the other. Now, in this delineation which I intend to make of a tyrant, all the lineaments, all the colours, will be found so naturally to correspond with the life, that it cannot but be doubted whether his Highness be the original or the copy; whether I have in drawing the tyrant represented him, or in representing him expressed a tyrant. And therefore, lest I should be suspected to deal insincerely with his Highness, and not to have applied these following characters, but made them, I shall not give you any of my own stamping, but such as I find in Plato, Aristotle, Tacitus, and his Highness's own evangelist, Machiavel.

1. Almost all tyrants have been first Captains and Generals for the people, under pretences of vindicating or defending their liberties. " Ut imperium evertant libertatem præferunt ; cum perverterunt, ipsam aggrediuntur," says Tacitus: to subvert the present Government they pretend liberty for the people ; when the Government is down they then invade that liberty themselves. This needs no application.

2. Tyrants accomplish their ends much more by fraud than force. Neither virtue nor force (says Machiavel) are so necessary to that purpose as "una astutia fortunata," a lucky craft ; which, says he, without force hath been often found sufficient, but never force without that. And in another place he tells us their way is " aggirare i cervelli degli huomini con astutia," &c. ; with cunning plausible pretences to impose upon men's understandings, and in the end they master those that had so little wit as to rely upon their faith and integrity. It is but unnecessary to say, that had not his Highness had a faculty to be fluent in his tears, and eloquent in his execrations ; had he not had spongy eyes, and a supple conscience ; and besides, to do with a people of great faith but little wit, his courage, and the rest of his moral virtues, with the help of his janissaries, had never been able so far to advance him out of the reach of justice that we should have need to call for any other hand to remove him but that of the hangman.

3. They abase all excellent persons, and rid out of the way all that have noble minds ; " et terræ filios extollunt," and advance sons of the earth. To put Aristotle into other words, they purge both Parliament and army, till they leave few or none there that have either honour or conscience, either wit, interest, or courage, to oppose their designs ; and in these purgations (saith Plato) tyrants do quite contrary to physicians, for they purge us of our humours, but tyrants of our spirits.

4. They dare suffer no assemblies, not so much as horse-races.

5. In all places they have their spies and dilaters ; that is, they have their Broughalls, their St. Johns (besides innumerable small spies), to appear discontented, and not to side with them, that under that disguise they may get trust and make discoveries. They likewise have their emissaries to send with forged letters. If any doubt this, let him send to Major-General Brown, and he will satisfy him.

6. They stir not without a guard, nor his Highness without his Lifeguard.

7. They impoverish the people, that they may want the power, if they have the will, to attempt anything against them. His Highness's way is by taxes excise, decimations, &c.

8. They make war to divert and busy the people, and besides, to have a pretence to raise moneys, and to make new levies, if they either distrust their old

forces, or think them not sufficient. The war with Spain serveth his Highness to this purpose, and upon no other justice was it begun at first, or still continued.

9. They will seem to honour and provide for good men—that is, if the ministers will be orthodox and flatter, if they will wrest and torture the Scriptures to prove his Government lawful, and furnish him with title, his Highness will likewise be then content to understand Scripture in their favour, and furnish them with tithes.

10. Things that are odious and distasteful they make others executioners of; and when the people are discontented, they appease them with sacrificing those ministers they employ. I leave it to his Highness's major-generals to ruminate a little upon this point.

11. In all things they pretend to be wonderful careful of the public, to give general accounts of the money they receive, which they pretend to be levied for the maintenance of the State and the prosecuting of the war. His Highness made an excellent comment upon this place of Aristotle in his speech to this Parliament.

12. All things set aside for religious uses they set to sale, that while those things last they may exact the less of the people. The Cavaliers would interpret this of the dean and chapter's lands.

13. They pretend inspirations from God, and

responses from oracles, to authorize what they do. His Highness hath been ever an enthusiast. And as Hugh Capet in taking the crown pretended to be admonished to it in a dream by St. Vallery and St. Richard, so I believe will his Highness do the same at the instigation of St. Henry and St. Richard, his two sons.

14. Lastly, above all things they pretend a love to God and religion. This Aristotle calls "Artium tyrannicarum potissimam," the surest and best of all the arts of tyrants; and we all know his Highness hath found it so by experience. He hath found, indeed, that in godliness there is great gain, and that preaching and praying well managed will obtain other kingdoms as well as that of heaven. His, indeed, have been pious arms, for he hath conquered most by those of the Church, by prayers and tears. But the truth is, were it not for our honour to be governed by one that can manage both the spiritual and temporal sword, and, Roman-like, to have our emperor our high-priest, we might have had preaching at a much cheaper rate, and it would have cost us but our tithes which now costs us all.

Other marks and rules there are mentioned by Aristotle to know tyrants by, but they being unsuitable to his Highness's actions, and impracticable by his temper, I insist not on them. As among other things, Aristotle would not have a tyrant insolent in his behaviour, nor strike people; but his Highness is naturally choleric, and must call men rogues, and go to cuffs. At last he concludes he should so fashion his manners, as neither to be really good nor absolutely bad, but half one, half the other. Now this half good is too great a proportion for his Highness, and much more than his temper will bear.

But to speak truths more seriously, and to conclude this first question: certainly whatever these characters make any man, it cannot be denied but his Highness is; and then if he be not a tyrant, we must confess we have no definition nor description of a tyrant left us, and may well imagine there is no such thing in Nature, and that it is only a notion and a name. But if there be such a beast, and we do at all believe what we see and feel, let us now inquire, according to the method we proposed, whether this be a beast of game that we are to give law to, or a beast of prey to destroy with all means which are allowable and fair?

In deciding this question authors very much differ, as far as it concerns supreme magistrates, who degenerate into tyrants. Some think they are to be borne with as bad parents, and place them in the number of those mischiefs that have no other cure but our patience. Others think they may be questioned by that supreme law of the people, safety; and that they are answerable to the people's representatives for the breach of their trust. But none of sober sense makes private persons judges of their actions, which were indeed to subvert all Government. But, on the other side, I find none (that have not been frighted or corrupted out of their reason) that have been so great enemies to common justice and the liberty of mankind as to give any kind of indemnity to a usurper, who can pretend no title but that of being stronger, nor challenge the people's obedience upon any other obligation but that of their necessity and fear. Such a person as one out of all bonds of human protection all men make the Ishmael, against whom is every man's hand as is his against every man. To him they give no more security than Cain, his fellow murderer and oppressor, promised to himself to be destroyed by him that found him first.

The reason why a tyrant's case is particular, and why, in that, every man hath that vengeance given him which in other cases is reserved to God and the magistrate, cannot be obscure if we rightly consider what a tyrant is, what his crimes are, and in what state he stands with the Commonwealth, and with every member of it. And certainly if we find him an enemy to all human society, and a subverter of all laws, and one that by the greatness of his villanies secures himself against all ordinary course of justice, we shall not at all think it strange if then he have no benefit from human society, no protection from the law, and if in his case justice dispenses with her forms. We are therefore to consider that the end for which men enter into society is not barely to live, which they may do dispersed, as other animals, but to live happily, and a life answerable to the dignity and excellency of their kind. Out of society this happiness is not to be had, for singly we are impotent and defective, unable to procure those things that are either of necessity or ornament for our lives, and as unable to defend and keep them when they are acquired. To remedy these defects we associate together, that what we can neither joy nor keep singly, by mutual benefits and assistances one of another we may be able to do both. We cannot possibly accomplish these ends if we submit not our passions and appetites to the laws of reason and justice. For the depravity of man's will makes him as unfit to live in society as his necessity makes him unable to live out of it. And if that perverseness be not regulated by laws, men's appetites to the same things, their avarice, their lust, their ambition would quickly make society as unsafe, or more, than solitude itself, and we should associate only to be nearer our misery and our ruin. That, therefore, by which we accomplish the ends of a sociable life, is our subjection and submission to laws; these are the nerves and sinews of every society or Commonwealth, without which they must necessarily dissolve and fall asunder. And, indeed, as Augustine says, those societies where law and justice is not are not Commonwealths or kingdoms, but "magna latrocinia," great confederacies of thieves and robbers. Those therefore that submit to no law are not to be reputed in the society of mankind, which cannot consist without a law. Therefore Aristotle saith, tyranny is against the law of Nature—that is, the law of human society in which human nature is preserved. For this reason they deny a tyrant to be "partem civitatis;" for every part is subject to the whole; and a citizen, says the same author, is he who is as well obliged to the duty of obeying as he is capable of the power of commanding. And indeed he does obey whilst he does command; that is, he obeys the laws, which, says Tully, "magistratibus præsunt, ut magistratus præsunt populo," are above the magistrates, as the magistrates are above the people. And, therefore, a tyrant that submits to no law, but his will and lust are the law by which he governs himself and others, is no magistrate, no citizen or member of any society, but an ulcer and a disease that destroys it; and if it be rightly considered, a Commonwealth by falling into a tyranny absolutely loses that name, and is actually another thing. "Non est civitas quæ unius est viri," saith Sophocles: that which is one man's is no city. For there is no longer king and people, or Parliament and people, but those names are changed (at least their natures) into masters and servants, lords and slaves; and "servorum non civitas erit sed magna familia," says Grotius; where all are slaves it is not a city, but a great family. And the truth is, we are all members of Whitehall, and when our master pleaseth he may send for us thither, and there bore through our ears at the door-posts. But to conclude: a tyrant, as we have said, being no part of a Commonwealth, not submitting to the laws of it, but making himself above all law, there is no reason he should have the protection that is due to a member of a Commonwealth, nor any defence from laws, that does acknowledge none. He is therefore in all reason to be reckoned in the number of those savage beasts that fall not with others into any herd, that have no other defence but their own strength, making a prey of all that is weaker, and, by the same justice, being a prey to all that is stronger than themselves.

In the next place, let it be considered that a tyrant making himself above all law, and defending his injustice by a strength which no power of magistrates is able to oppose, he becomes above all punishment, above all other justice than that he receives from the stroke of some generous hand. And, certainly, the safety of mankind were but ill provided for if there were no kind of justice to reach great villanies, but tyrants should be "immanitate scelerum tuti," secured by the greatness of their crimes. Our laws would be then but cobwebs indeed, made only to catch flies, but not to hold wasps or hornets; and it might be then said of all Commonwealths what was said of Athens: that there only small thieves were hanged, but the great ones were free, and condemned the rest. But he that will secure himself of all hands must know he secures himself from none; he that flies justice in the court must expect to find it in the street, and he that goes armed against every man arms every man against himself. "Bellum est in eos, qui judiciis coerceri non possunt," says Cicero; we have war with those against whom we can have no law. The same author, "cum duo sint decertandi genera," &c. There being two ways of deciding differences: the one by judgment and arbitration, the other by force; the one proper to men, the other to beasts; we must have recourse to the latter when the former cannot be obtained. And, certainly, by the law of Nature, "ubi cessat judicium," when no justice can be had, every man may be his own magistrate, and do justice for himself. For the law, says Grotius, that forbids me to pursue my right but by a course of law, certainly supposes "ubi copia est judicii," where law and justice is to be had; otherwise, that law were a defence for injuries, not one against them, and, quite contrary to the nature of all laws, would become the protection of the guilty against the innocent, not of the innocent against the guilty Now, as it is contrary to the laws of God and

Nature that men who are partial to themselves, and therefore unjust to others, should be their own judges where others are to be had, so it is contrary to the law of Nature and the common safety of mankind that, when the law can have no place, men should be forbidden to repel force by force, and so to be left without all defence and remedy against injuries. God himself left not the slave without remedy against the cruel master; and what analogy can it hold with reason, that the slave, that is but his master's money and but part of his household-stuff, should find redress against the injuries and insolences of an imperious master, and a free people who have no superior but their God should have none at all against the injustice and oppression of a barbarous tyrant; and were not the incongruity fully as great, that the law of God permitting every man to kill a thief if he took him breaking open his house in the night, because then it might be supposed he could not bring him to justice; but a tyrant, that is the common robber of mankind, and whom no law can take hold on, his person should be "sacrosancta, cui nihil sacrum aut sanctum," to whom nothing is sacred, nothing inviolable; but the vulgar judge ridiculously like themselves. The glitter of things dazzles their eyes, and they judge of them by their appearances, and the colours that are put on them. For what can be more absurd in Nature, and contrary to all common sense, than to call him thief, and kill him that comes alone or with a few to rob me, and to call him Lord Protector, and obey him, that robs me with regiments and troops? As if to rove with two or three ships were to be a pirate, but with fifty an admiral? But if it be the number of adherents only, not the cause, that makes the difference between a robber and a Protector, I wish that number were defined, that we might know where the thief ends and the prince begins, and be able to distinguish between a robbery and a tax. But, surely, no Englishman can be ignorant that it is his birthright to be master of his own estate, and that none can command any part of it but by his own grant and consent, either made expressly by himself, or virtually by a Parliament. All other ways are mere robberies in other names: "Auferre, trucidare, rapere, falsis nominibus imperium, atque ubi solitudinem faciunt, pacem appellant;" to rob, to extort, to murder, tyrants falsely call to govern, and to make desolation they call to settle peace. In every assessment we are robbed: the excise is robbery, the custom is robbery, and without doubt, whenever it is prudent, it is always lawful to kill the thieves whom we can bring to no other justice. And not only lawful, and to do ourselves right, but glorious, and to deserve of mankind, to free the world of that common robber, that universal pirate, under whom and for whom these lesser beasts prey. This firebrand I would have any way extinguished, this ulcer I would have any hand to lance. And I cannot doubt but God will suddenly sanctify some hand to do it, and bring down that bloody and deceitful man, who lives not only to the misery, but the infamy of our nation.

I should have reason to be much less confident of the justice of this opinion if it were new, and only grounded upon collections and interpretations of my own: but herein, if I am deceived, I shall however have the excuse to have been drawn into that error by the examples that are left us by the greatest and most virtuous, and the opinions of the wisest and gravest men that have left their memoirs to posterity. Out of the great plenty of confirmations I could bring for this opinion from examples and authorities, I shall select a very few; for manifest truths have not need of those supports, and I have as little mind to tire myself as my reader.

First, therefore, a usurper, that by only force possesseth himself of government, and by force only keeps it, is yet in the state of war with every man, says the learned Grotius; and therefore everything is lawful against him that is lawful against an open enemy, whom every private man hath a right to kill. "Hostis hostem occidere volui," says Scævola to Porsenna, when he was taken, after he had failed in his attempt to kill him; I am an enemy, and an enemy I would have killed, which every man hath a right to do.

"Contra publicos hostes, et majestatis reos, omnis homo miles est," says Tertullian; against common enemies, and those that are traitors to the Commonwealth, every man is a soldier. This opinion the most celebrated nations have approved, both by their laws and practices. The Grecians, as Xenophon tells us, who suffered not murderers to come into their temples, in those very temples they erected statues to those that killed tyrants, thinking it fit to place their deliverances amongst their gods. Cicero was an eye-witness of the honours that were done such men, "Græci homines," &c. The Greeks, saith he, attribute the honours of the gods to those that killed tyrants. What have I seen in Athens, and other cities of Greece! What religion paid to such men! what songs! what eulogies! by which they are consecrated to immortality, and almost deified! In Athens, by Solon's law, death was not only decreed for the tyrant that oppressed the State, but for all those that took any charge or did bear any office while the tyranny remained. And Plato tells us the ordinary course they took with tyrants in Greece. If, says he, the tyrant cannot be expelled by accusing him to the citizens, then by secret practices they dispatch him.

Amongst the Romans the Valerian law was, "Si quis injussu populi," &c. Whosoever took magistracy upon him without the command of the people, it was lawful for any man to kill him. Plutarch makes this law more severe: "Ut injudicatum occidere eum liceret, qui dominatum concupisceret;" that it was lawful by that law, before any judgment passed, to kill him that but aspired to tyranny. Likewise the Consular law, which was made after the suppression of the tyranny of the Decemvirate, made it lawful to kill any man that went about to create magistrates, " sine provocatione," &c., without reference and appeal to the people. By these laws, and innumerable testimonies of authors, it appears that the Romans, with the rest of their philosophy, had learned from the Grecians what was the natural remedy against a tyrant: nor did they honour those less that durst apply it, who, as Polybius says, speaking of conspiracies against tyrants, were not "deterrimi civium, sed generosissimi quique, et maximi animi;" not the worst and meanest of the citizens, but the generous, and those of greatest virtue. So were most of those that conspired against Julius Cæsar. He himself thought Brutus worthy to succeed him in the empire of the world; and Cicero, who had the title of Pater Patriæ, if he were not conscious of the design, yet he at least affected the honour of being thought so. "Quæ enim res unquam," &c. What act, says he, O Jupiter, more glorious, more worthy of eternal memory, hath been done not only in this city, but in the whole world! In this design, as the Trojan horse, I willingly suffer myself to be included with the princes. In the same place he tells us what all virtuous Romans thought of the fact as well as he. "Omnes boni, quantum in ipsis fiat, Cæsarem occiderunt: aliis consilium, aliis animus, aliis occasio defuit, voluntas nemini;" all good men, saith he, as much as in them lay, killed Cæsar: some wanted capacity, some courage, others opportunity, but none the will to do it. But yet we have not declared the extent of their severity against a tyrant. They exposed him to fraud as well as force, and left him no security in oaths and compacts, that neither law nor religion might defend him that violated both. "Cum tyranno Romanis nulla fides, nulla juris jurandi religio," saith Brutus in Appian; with a tyrant the Romans think no faith to be kept, observe no religion of an oath. Seneca gives the reason: "Quia quicquid erat, quo mihi cohæreret," &c; for whatever there was of mutual obligation betwixt us, his destroying the laws of human society hath dissolved. So these that thought that there was in "hostem nefas," that a villany might be committed against an enemy; these that professed, "non minus juste quam fortiter arma gerere," to manage their arms with justice as well as courage; these that thought faith was to be kept even with the perfidious, yet they thought a tyrant could receive no injustice but to be let live, and that the most lawful way to destroy him was the readiest, no matter whether by force or fraud; for against beasts of prey men use the toil and the net, as well as the spear and the lance. But so great was their detestation of a tyrant, that it made some take their opinions from their passions, and vent things which they could but ill justify to their morality; they thought a tyrant had so absolutely forfeited all title to humanity, and all kind of protection they could give him or his, that they left his wife without any other guard for her chastity but age and deformity, and thought it not adultery what was committed with her. Many more testimonies might I bring, for it is harder to make choice than to find plenty; but I shall conclude with authorities that are much more authentic, and examples which we may much more safely imitate.

The law of God itself decreed certain death to that man that would do presumptuously, and admit to no decision of justice. Who can read this and think a tyrant ought to live? But certainly neither that, nor any other law, were to any effect, if there were no way to put it in execution; but in a tyrant's case process and citation have no place, and if we will only have formal remedies against him we are sure to have none. There is small hope of justice where the malefactor hath a power to condemn the judge.

All remedy, therefore, against a tyrant is Ehud's dagger, without which all our laws were fruitless and we helpless. This is that high court of justice where Moses brought the Egyptian, whither Ehud brought Eglon, Samson the Philistines, Samuel Agag, and Jehoiada the she-tyrant Athaliah.

Let us a little consider in particular these several examples, and see whether they may be proportioned to our purpose.

First, as to the case of Moses and the Egyptian. Certainly every Englishman hath as much call as Moses, and more cause than he, to slay this Egyptian, that is always laying on burdens, and always smiting both our brethren and ourselves. For as to his call, he had no other that we read of but the necessity his brother stood in of his help. He looked on his brethren's burdens, and, seeing an Egyptian smiting a Hebrew, knowing he was out of the reach of all other kind of justice, he slew him.

Certainly this was and is as lawful for any man to do as it was for Moses, who was then but a private man, and had no authority for what he did but what the law of Nature gives every man, to oppose force to force, and to make justice where he finds none. As to the cause of that action we have much more to say than Moses had: he saw one Hebrew smitten, we many Englishmen murdered; he saw his brethren's burdens and their blows, we our brethren's burdens, imprisonments, and deaths. Now sure if it were lawful for Moses to kill that Egyptian that oppressed one man, being there was no way to procure an ordinary course of justice against him, it cannot be but absurd to think it unlawful to kill him that oppresses a whole nation, and one that justice as little reaches as it defends.

The example of Ehud shows us the natural, and almost the only remedy against a tyrant, and the way to free an oppressed people from the slavery of an insulting Moabite. It is done by prayers and tears, with the help of a dagger: by crying to the Lord, and the left hand of an Ehud. Devotion and action go well together; for believe it, a tyrant is not of that kind of devil that is to be cast out by only fasting and prayer. And here the Scripture shows us what the Lord thought a fit message to send a tyrant from himself, a dagger of a cubit in his belly; and every worthy man that desires to be an Ehud, a deliverer of his country, will strive to be the messenger.

We may here likewise observe in this, and many places of Judges, that when the Israelites fell to idolatry, which of all sins certainly is one of the greatest, God Almighty, to proportion the punishment and the offence, still delivered them into the hands of tyrants, which sure is one of the greatest of all plagues.

In the story of Samson it is manifest that the

denying him his wife, and after the burning her and her father, which, though they were great, yet were but private injuries, he took for sufficient grounds to make war upon the Philistines, being himself but a private man, and not only not assisted but opposed by his servile countrymen. He knew what the law of Nature allowed him, where other laws have no place; and thought it sufficient justification for smiting the Philistines hip and thigh, to answer for himself that, as they did unto him, so had he done unto them.

Now, that which was lawful for Samson to do against many oppressors, why is it unlawful for us to do against one? Are our injuries less? Our friends and relations are daily murdered before our faces. Have we other ways for reparation? Let them be named, and I am silenced. But if we have none, the firebrands or the jawbone, the first weapons our just fury can lay hold on may certainly be lawfully employed against that uncircumcised Philistine that oppresses us. We have, too, the opposition and discouragements that Samson had, and therefore have the more need of his courage and resolution. As he had the men of Judah, so we have the men of Levi, crying to us out of the pulpit, as from the top of the rock Etam, Know you not that the Philistine is a ruler over you? The truth is, they would fain make him so, and bind us with Samson in new cords; but we hope they will become as flax, and that they will either loose from our hands, or we shall have the courage to cut them.

Upon the same grounds of retaliation did Samuel do justice with his own hand upon the tyrant Agag. As thy sword, says the prophet, hath made women childless, so shall thy mother be childless amongst women ; nor is there any law more natural, and more just.

How many mothers has our Agag for his own ambition made childless? How many children fatherless? How many have this reason to hew this Amalekite in pieces before the Lord? And let his own relations, and all theirs that are confederates with him, beware lest men come at last to revenge their own relations in them. They make many a woman husbandless, many a father childless. Their wives may come at last to know what it is to want a husband, and themselves to lose their children. Let them remember what their great apostle Machiavel tells them, that in contestations for the preserving their liberty people many times use moderation ; but when they come to vindicate it, their rigour exceeds all mean ; like beasts that have been kept up, and are afterwards let loose, they always are more fierce and cruel. To conclude with the example Jehoiada hath left us : six years he hid the right heir of the crown in the house of the Lord, and without all doubt, amongst the rest of God's services there, he was all that time contriving the destruction of the tyrant, that had aspired to the crown by the destruction of those that had the right to it. Jehoiada had no pretence to authorize this action but the equity and justice of the act itself. He pretended no immediate command from God for what he did, nor any authority from the Sanhedrin, and therefore any man might have done what Jehoiada did as lawfully that could have done it as effectually. Now what citation was given to Athaliah? What appearance was she called to before any court of justice. Her fact was her trial; she was without any expostulation taken forth of the ranges, and only let live till she got out of the Temple, that that holy place might not be defiled by the blood of a tyrant, which was fitter to be shed on a dunghill, and so they slew her at the Horse-gate. And by the king's house, the very Whitehall, where she had caused the blood royal to be spilt, and which herself had so long unjustly possessed, there by Providence did she receive her punishment, where she had acted so great a part of her crimes. How the people approved of this glorious action of destroying a tyrant, this chapter tells us at the last verse. And all the people of the land rejoiced, and the city was quiet, after they had slain Athaliah with the sword. And that it may appear they no less honoured the authors of such actions than other nations did, as in his lifetime they obeyed Jehoiada as a king, so after his death, for the good he had done in Israel (saith the Scripture) they buried him amongst the kings.

I must not conclude this story without observing that Jehoiada commanded that whosoever followed Athaliah should be put to death, letting us see what they deserve that are confederates with tyrants and will side with them, and but appear to defend them, or allow them. His Highness's Council, his Junto, and the agas of his janissaries, may, if they please, take notice of this, and repent, lest they likewise perish. And likewise his Highness's chaplains and triers, who are to admit none into the ministry that will preach liberty with the Gospel, may, if they think fit, observe that with the tyrant fell Mattan, the priest of Baal. And, indeed, none but Baal's priests will preach for tyrants. And certainly those priests that sacrifice to our Baal, our idol of a magistrate, deserve as well to be hanged before their pulpits as ever Mattan did to fall before his altars.

I should think now I had said much more than enough to the second question, and should come to the third and last I proposed in my method, but I meet with two objections lying in my way. The first is, that these examples out of Scripture are of men that were inspired of God, and that therefore they had that call and authority for their actions which we cannot pretend to, so that it would be unsafe for us to draw their actions into examples except we had likewise their justification to allege.

The other objection is, that there being now no opposition made to the government of his Highness, that the people following their callings and traffic at home and abroad, making use of the laws and appealing to his Highness's courts of justice, that all this argues the people's tacit consent to the government, and that therefore now it is to be reputed lawful and the people's obedience voluntary.

To the first I answer with learned Milton, that if God commanded these things it is a sign they were lawful, and are commendable. But, secondly, as I observed in the relations of the examples themselves, neither Samson nor Samuel alleged any other cause or reason for what they did but retaliation, and the apparent justice of the actions themselves. Nor had God appeared to Moses in the bush when he slew the Egyptian; nor did Jehoiada allege any prophetical authority or other call to do what he did, but that common call which all men have, to do all actions of justice that are within their power when the ordinary course of justice ceases.

To the second my answer is, that if commerce and pleadings were enough to argue the people's consent, and give tyranny the name of government, there was never yet any tyranny of many weeks' standing in this world. Certainly, we then extremely wrong Caligula and Nero in calling them tyrants, and they were rebels that conspired against them, except we will believe that all the while they reigned in Rome they kept their shops shut, and opened not their temples or their courts. We are likewise with no less absurdity to imagine that the whole eighteen years' time which Israel served Eglon, and six years that Athaliah reigned, that the Israelites quite desisted from traffic, pleadings, and all public acts; otherwise Ehud and Jehoiada were both traitors, the one for killing his king, the other his queen.

Having showed what a tyrant is, his marks and practices, I can scarce persuade myself to say anything to that I made my third question, whether the removing him is like to prove of advantage to the Commonwealth or not? For methinks it is to inquire whether it is better the man die, or the imposthume be lanced, or the gangrened limb be cut off? But yet there be some whose cowardice and avarice furnish them with some arguments to the contrary, and they would fain make the world believe that to be base and degenerate is to be cautious and prudent; and what is in truth a servile fear they falsely call a Christian patience. It will not be therefore amiss to make appear that there is indeed that necessity which we think there is of saving the vineyard of the Commonwealth, if possible, by destroying the wild boar that is broke into it.

We have already shown that it is lawful, and now we shall see whether it is expedient. First, I have already told you that to be under a tyrant is not to be a Commonwealth, but a great family, consisting of master and slaves. "Vis servorum nulla est usquam civitas," says an old poet; a number of slaves makes not a city. So that whilst this monster lives we are not members of a Commonwealth, but only his living tools and instruments, which he may employ to what use he pleases. "Servi tua est fortuna, ratio ad te nihil," says another; thy condition is a slave's, thou art not to inquire a reason. Nor must we think we can continue long in the condition of slaves, and not degenerate into the habits and temper that is natural to that condition: our minds will grow low with our fortune, and, by being accustomed to live like slaves, we shall become unfit to be anything else. "Etiam fera animalia si clausa teneas virtutis obliviscuntur," says Tacitus; the fiercest creatures by long constraint lose their courage. And says Sir Francis Bacon, the blessing of Issachar and that of Judah falls not upon one people, to be asses couching under burdens and to have the spirit of lions. And with their courage it is no wonder if they lose their fortune, as the effect with the cause, and act as ignominiously abroad as they suffer at home. It is Machiavel's observation that the Roman armies, that were always victorious under Consuls, all the while they were under the slavery of the Decemviri never prospered. And certainly people have reason to fight but faintly where they are to gain the victory against themselves, when every success shall be a confirmation of their slavery and a new link to their chain.

But we shall not only lose our courage, which is a useless and an unsafe virtue under a tyrant, but by degrees we shall, after the example of our master, all turn perfidious, deceitful, irreligious, flatterers, and whatever else is villanous and infamous in mankind. See but to what a degree we are come to already. Can there any oath be found so fortified by all religious ties which we easily find not a distinction to break, when either profit or danger persuades us to it? Do we remember any engagements? Or if we do, have we any shame to break them? Can any man think with patience upon what we have professed, when he sees what we vilely do and tamely suffer? What have we of nobility amongst us but the name, the luxury, and the vices of it? Poor wretches! These that now carry that title are so far from having any of the virtues that should grace, and indeed give them their titles, that they have not so much as the generous vices that attend greatness: they have lost all ambition and indignation. As for our ministers, what have they, or indeed desire they, of their calling, but the tithes? How do these horrid prevaricators search for distinctions to piece contrary oaths? How do they wrack scriptures for flatteries, and impudently apply them to his monstrous Highness? What is the city but a great tame beast, that eats and carries, and cares not who rides it? What's the thing called a Parliament but a mock? Composed of a people that are only suffered to sit there because they are known to have no virtue, after the exclusion of all others that were but suspected to have any, what are they but pimps of tyranny, who are only employed to draw in the people to prostitute their liberty? What will not the army fight for? What will they not fight against? What are they but janissaries? Slaves themselves, and making all others so? What are the people in general but knaves, fools, and cowards; principled for ease, vice and slavery? This our temper, his tyranny hath brought us to already, and if it continues the little virtue that is yet left to stock the nation must totally extinguish, and then his Highness hath completed his work of reformation. And the truth is till then his Highness cannot be secure. He must not endure virtue, for that will not endure him. He that will maintain tyranny must kill Brutus, says Machiavel. A tyrant, says Plato, must dispatch all virtuous persons or he cannot be safe; so that he is brought to that unhappy necessity, either to live among base and wicked persons, or not to live at all.

Nor must we expect any cure from our patience. "Ingannonsi gli huomini," says Machiavel; "credendo con la humilità vincere la superbia;" men deceive themselves that think to mollify arrogancy with humility; a tyrant is never modest but when he is weak; it is in the winter of his fortune when this serpent bites not. We must not therefore suffer ourselves to be cozened with hopes of his amendment: for "nemo unquam Imperium flagitio quæsitum, bonis artibus exercuit;" never did any man manage that government with justice that got it by villany. The longer the tyrant lives, the more the tyrannical humour increases in him, says Plato, like those beasts that grow more curst as they grow old. New occasions daily happen that necessitate them to new mischiefs, and he must defend one villany with another.

But suppose the contrary of all this, and that his Highness were "vi dominationis convulsus, et mutatus," changed to the better by great fortune, of which he yet gives no symptoms, what notwithstanding could be more miserable, than to have no other security for our liberty, no other law for our safety, than the will of a man, though the most just living? We have all our beast within us, and whosoever, says Aristotle, is governed by a man without a law is governed by a man and by a beast. "Etiam si non sit molestus, Dominus; tamen est miserrimum posse si velit," says Tully; though a master does not tyrannize, yet it is a miserable thing that it is in his power to do so if he will. If he be good, so was

Nero for five years, and how shall we be secure that he will not change? Besides, the power that is allowed to a good man we may be sure will be claimed and taken by an ill. And therefore it hath been the custom of good princes to abridge their own power, it may be distrusting themselves, but certainly fearing their successors, to the chance of whose being virtuous they would not hazard the welfare of their people. An unlimited power therefore is to be trusted to none, which, if it does not find a tyrant, commonly makes one; or, if one uses it modestly, it is no argument that others will; and therefore Augustus Cæsar must have no greater power given him than you would have Tiberius take. Cicero's moderation is to be trusted with a consideration that there are others to be Consuls as well as he.

But before I press this business further, if it needs be any further pressed, that we should endeavour to rescue the honour, the virtue and liberty of our nation, I shall answer to some few objections that have occurred to me. This I shall do very briefly.

Some I find of a strange opinion, that it were a generous and a noble action to kill his Highness in the field, but to do it privately they think it unlawful, but know not why. As if it were not generous to apprehend a thief till his sword were drawn, and he in a posture to defend himself and kill me. But these people do not consider, that whosoever is possessed of power any time will be sure to engage so many either in guilt or profit, or both, that to go about to throw him out by open force will very much hazard the total ruin of the Commonwealth. A tyrant is a devil, that tears the body in the exorcising; and they are all of Caligula's temper, that if they could they would have the whole frame of Nature fall with them. It is an opinion that deserves no other refutation than the manifest absurdity of itself, that it would be lawful for me to destroy a tyrant with hazard, blood, and confusion, but not without.

Another objection, and more common, is the fear of what may succeed if his Highness were removed. One would think the world were bewitched. I am fallen into a ditch, where I shall certainly perish if I lie, but I refuse to be helped out for fear of falling into another; I suffer a certain misery for fear of a contingent one, and let the disease kill me, because there is hazard in the cure. Is not this that ridiculous policy, "Ne moriar, mori;" to die for fear of dying. Sure it is frenzy not to desire a change, when we are sure we cannot be worse: "et non incurrere in pericula, ubi quiescenti paria metuuntur;" and not then to hazard when the danger and the mischiefs are the same in lying still.

Hitherto I have spoken in general to all Englishmen, now I address my discourse particularly to those that certainly best deserve that name, ourselves, that have fought, however unfortunately, for our liberties under this tyrant; and in the end, cozened by his oaths and tears, have purchased nothing but our slavery with the price of our blood. To us particularly it belongs to bring this monster to justice, whom he hath made the instruments of his villany, and sharers in the curse and detestation that is due to himself from all good men. Others only have their liberty to vindicate, we our liberty and our honour. We engaged to the people with him, and to the people for him, and from our hands they may justly expect a satisfaction of punishment, being they cannot have that of performance. What the people at present endure, and posterity shall suffer, will be all laid at our doors : for only we under God have the power to pull down this Dagon which we have set up. And if we do it not, all mankind will repute us approvers of all the villanies he hath done, and authors of all to come. Shall we that would not endure a king attempting tyranny, shall we suffer a professed tyrant? We that resisted the lion assailing us, shall we submit to the wolf tearing us? If there be no remedy to be found we have great reason to exclaim : " Utinam te potius (Carole) retinuissemus quam hunc habuissemus, non quod ulla sit optanda servitus, sed quod ex dignitate Domini minus turpis est conditio servi;" we wish we had rather endured thee (O Charles) than have been condemned to this mean tyrant; not that we desire any kind of slavery, but that the quality of the master something graces the condition of the slave.

But if we consider it rightly what our duty, our engagements, and our honour exact from us, both our safety and our interest oblige us to, and it is as unanswerable in us to discretion, as it is to virtue, to let this viper live. For first, he knows very well it is only we that have the power to hurt him, and therefore of us he will take any course to secure himself: he is conscious to himself how falsely and perfidiously he hath dealt with us, and therefore he will always fear that from our revenge which he knows he hath so well deserved.

Lastly, he knows our principles, how directly contrary they are to that arbitrary power he must govern by, and therefore he may reasonably suspect that we that have already ventured our lives against tyranny will always have the will, when we have the opportunity, to do the same again.

These considerations will easily persuade him to secure himself of us, if we prevent him not, and secure ourselves of him. He reads in his practice of piety, "chi diviene patron," &c.: he that makes himself master of a city that hath been accustomed to liberty, if he destroys it not, he must expect to be destroyed by it. And we may read too in the same author, and believe him, that those that are the occasion that one becomes powerful he always ruins them if they want the wit and courage to secure themselves.

Now as to our interest, we must never expect that he will ever trust those that he hath provoked and feared; he will be sure to keep us down, lest we should pluck down him. It is the rule that tyrants observe when they are in power, never to make much use of those that helped them to it; and indeed it is their interest and security not to do it, for those that have been the authors of their greatness, being conscious of their own merit, they are bold with the tyrant, and less industrious to please him. They think all he can do for them is their due, and still they expect more; and when they fail in their expectations—as it is impossible to satisfy them—their disappointment makes them discontented, and their discontent is dangerous. Therefore all tyrants follow the example of Dionysius, who was said to use his friends as he did his bottles: when he had use for them he kept them by him, and when he had none, that they should not trouble him and lie in his way, he hung them up.

But, to conclude this already over-long paper: let every man to whom God hath given the spirit of wisdom and courage be persuaded by his honour, his safety, his own good, and his country's, and indeed the duty he owes to his generation and to mankind, to endeavour by all rational means to free the world of this pest. Let not other nations have the occasion to think so meanly of us as if we resolved to sit still and have our ears bored, or that any discouragement or disappointments can ever make us desist from attempting our liberty, till we have purchased it, either by this monster's death or by our own. Our nation is not yet so barren of virtue that we want noble examples to follow amongst ourselves. The brave Sindercombe hath shown as great a mind as any old Rome could boast of; and had he lived there his name had been registered with Brutus and Cato, and he had had his statues as well as they.

But I will not have so sinister an opinion of ourselves, as little generosity as slavery hath left us, as to think so great a virtue can want its monuments even amongst us. Certainly in every virtuous mind there are statues reared to Sindercombe. Whenever we read the elegies of those that have died for their country; when we admire those great examples of magnanimity that have tired tyrants' cruelties; when we extol their constancies, whom neither bribes nor terrors could make betray their friends; it is then we erect Sindercombe's statues, and grave him monuments, where all that can be said of a great and noble mind we justly make an epitaph for him. And though the tyrant caused him to be smothered, lest the people should hinder an open murder, yet he will never be able either to smother his memory or his own villany. His poison was but a poor and common device, to impose only on those that understood not tyrants' practices, and are unacquainted, if any be, with his cruelties and falsehoods. He may therefore if he please take away the stake from Sindercombe's grave, and if he have a mind it should be known how he died, let him send thither the pillows and feather-beds with which Barkstead and his hangman smothered him. But, to conclude: let not this monster think himself the more secure that he hath suppressed one great spirit; he may be confident that "longus post illum sequitur ordo idem petentium decus."

There is a great roll behind, even of those that are in his own muster-rolls, that are ambitious of the name of the deliverers of their country; and they know what the action is that will purchase it. His bed, his table, is not secure; and he stands in need of other guards to defend him against his own. Death and destruction pursue him wheresoever he goes: they follow him everywhere, like his fellow-travellers, and at last they will come upon him like armed men. Darkness is hid in his secret places, a fire not blown shall consume him; it shall go ill with him that is left in his tabernacle. He shall flee from the iron weapon, and a bow of steel shall strike him through, because he hath oppressed and forsaken the poor, because he hath violently taken away a house which he builded not. We may be confident, and so may he, that ere long all this will be accomplished : for the triumphing of the wicked is but short, and the joy of the hypocrite but for a moment. Though his Excellency mount up to the heavens, and his head reacheth unto the clouds, yet he shall perish for ever like his own dung. They that have seen him shall say, Where is he?

THE SHORTEST WAY

WITH

THE DISSENTERS;

OR,

PROPOSALS FOR THE ESTABLISHMENT OF THE CHURCH.

THE

Shortest Way with the Dissenters;

OR, PROPOSALS FOR THE ESTABLISHMENT OF THE CHURCH.

SIR ROGER L'ESTRANGE tells us a story, in his collection of fables, of the cock and the horses. The cock was gotten to roost in the stable, among the horses, and there being no racks or other conveniences for him, it seems he was forced to roost upon the ground. The horses jostling about for room, and putting the cock in danger of his life, he gives them this grave advice: " Pray, gentlefolks, let us stand still, for fear we should tread upon one another."

There are some people in the world, who, now they are unperched, and reduced to an equality with other people, and under strong and very just apprehensions of being further treated as they deserve, begin, with Æsop's cock, to preach up peace and union, and the Christian duties of moderation, forgetting that when they had the power in their hands those graces were strangers in their gates.

It is now near fourteen years that the glory and peace of the purest and most flourishing Church in the world has been eclipsed, buffeted, and disturbed by a sort of men whom God in his providence has suffered to insult over her, and bring her down. These have been the days of her humiliation and tribulation : she has borne with an invincible patience the reproach of the wicked, and God has at last heard her prayers, and delivered her from the oppression of the stranger.

And, now they find their day is over, their power gone, and the throne of this nation possessed by a royal, English, true, and ever-constant member of and friend to the Church of England; now they find that they are in danger of the Church of England's just resentments ; now they cry out peace, union, forbearance, and charity, as if the Church had not too long harboured her enemies under her wing, and nourished the viperous brood, till they hiss and fly in the face of the mother that cherished them.

No, gentlemen, the time of mercy is past, your day of grace is over ; you should have practised peace, and moderation, and charity, if you expected any yourselves.

We have heard none of this lesson for fourteen years past: we have been huffed and bullied with your Act of Toleration; you have told us that you are the Church established by law, as well as others; have set up your canting synagogues at our church-doors, and the Church and members have been loaded with reproaches, with oaths, associations, abjurations, and what not. Where has been the mercy, the forbearance, the charity you have shown to tender consciences of the Church of England, that could not take oaths as fast as you made them; that having sworn allegiance to their lawful and rightful King, could not dispense with that oath, their King being still alive, and swear to your new hodge-podge of a Dutch Government? These have been turned out of their livings, and they and their families left to starve; their estates double taxed, to carry on a war they had no hand in, and you got nothing by. What account can you give of the multitudes you have forced to comply, against their consciences, with your new sophistical politics, who, like new converts in France, sin because they cannot starve? And, now the tables are turned upon you, you must not be persecuted; it is not a Christian spirit!

You have butchered one king, deposed another king, and made a mock king of a third; and yet you could have the face to expect to be employed and trusted by the fourth. Anybody that did not know the temper of your party, would stand amazed at the impudence as well as folly, to think of it.

Your management of your Dutch monarch, whom you reduced to a mere King of Cl———s, is enough to give any future princes such an idea of your principles as to warn them sufficiently from coming into your clutches; and, God be thanked! the Queen is out of your hands, knows you, and will have a care of you.

There is no doubt but the supreme authority of a nation has in itself a power, and a right to that power, to execute the laws upon any part of that nation it governs. The execution of the known laws of the land, and that with but a gentle hand neither, was all that the fanatical party of this land have ever called persecution; this they have magnified to a height, that the sufferings of the Huguenots in France were not to be compared with. Now, to execute the known laws of a nation upon those who transgress them, after voluntarily consenting to the making those laws, can never be called persecution, but justice. But justice is always violence to the party offending, for every man is innocent in his own eyes. The first execution of the laws against Dissenters in England was in the days of King James the First. And what did it amount to? Truly, the worst they suffered was, at their own request, to let them go to New England, and erect a new colony, and give them great privileges, grants, and suitable powers, keep them under protection, and defend them against all invaders, and receive no taxes or revenue from them. This was the cruelty of the Church of England! Fatal lenity! It was the ruin of that excellent prince, King Charles the First. Had King James sent all the Puritans in England away to the West Indies, we had been a national, unmixed Church; the Church of England had been kept undivided and entire.

To requite the lenity of the father, they take up arms against the son: conquer, pursue, take, imprison, and at last put to death the anointed of God, and destroy the very being and nature of government, setting up a sordid impostor, who had neither title to govern nor understanding to manage, but supplied that want with power, bloody and desperate councils and craft, without conscience.

Had not King James the First withheld the full execution of the laws, had he given them strict justice, he had cleared the nation of them, and the consequences had been plain: his son had never been murdered by them, nor the monarchy overwhelmed. It was too much mercy shown them was the ruin of his posterity, and the ruin of the nation's peace. One would think the Dissenters should not have the face to believe that we are to be wheedled and canted into peace and toleration, when they know that they have once requited us with a civil war, and once with an intolerable and unrighteous persecution for our former civility.

Nay, to encourage us to be easy with them, it is apparent that they never had the upper hand of the Church but they treated her with all the severity, with all the reproach and contempt as was possible. What peace and what mercy did they show the loyal gentry of the Church of England in the time of their triumphant Commonwealth? How did they put all the gentry of England to ransom, whether they were actually in arms for the King or not, making people compound for their estates, and starve their families? How did they treat the clergy of the Church of England? Sequestered the ministers, devoured the patrimony of the Church, and divided the spoil, by sharing the Church lands among their soldiers, and turning her clergy out to starve. Just such measure as they have meted should be measured them again.

Charity and love is the known doctrine of the Church of England, and it is plain she has put it in practice towards the Dissenters, even beyond what they ought, till she has been wanting to herself and, in effect, unkind to her own sons, particularly in the too much lenity of King James the First, mentioned before. Had he so rooted the Puritans from the face of the land, which he had an opportunity early to have done, they had not had the power to vex the Church, as since they have done.

In the days of King Charles the Second, how did the Church reward their bloody doings? With lenity and mercy. Except the barbarous regicides of the pretended Court of Justice, not a soul suffered for all the blood in an unnatural war. King Charles came in all mercy and love, cherished them, preferred them, employed them, withheld the rigour of the law, and oftentimes, even against the advice of his Parliament, gave them liberty of conscience. And how did they requite him? With the villanous contrivance to depose and murder him and his successor at the Rye Plot!

King James, as if mercy was the inherent quality of the family, began his reign with unusual favour to them; nor could their joining with the Duke of Monmouth against him move him to do himself justice upon them; but that mistaken Prince thought to win them by gentleness and love, proclaimed a universal liberty to them, and rather discountenanced the Church of England than them. How they requited him all the world knows.

The late reign is too fresh in the memory of all the world to need a comment; how, under pretence of joining with the Church in redressing some grievances, they pushed things to that extremity, in conjunction with some mistaken gentlemen, as to depose the late King, as if the grievance of the nation could not have been redressed but by the absolute ruin of the Prince. Here is an instance of their temper, their peace and charity. To what height they carried themselves during the reign of a king of their own; how they crept into all places of trust and profit; how they insinuated into the favour of the King, and were at first preferred to the highest places in the nation; how they engrossed the Ministry, and, above all, how pitifully they managed, is too plain to need any remarks.

But particularly their mercy and charity, the spirit of union, they tell us so much of, has been remarkable in Scotland. If any man would see the spirit of a Dissenter, let him look into Scotland. There they made entire conquest of the Church, trampled down the sacred orders, and suppressed the Episcopal government, with an absolute and, as they suppose, irretrievable victory, though it is possible they may find themselves mistaken. Now it would be a very proper question to ask their impudent advocate, the *Observator*: Pray how much mercy and favour did the members of the Episcopal Church find in Scotland from the Scotch Presbyterian Government? and I shall undertake for the Church of England that the Dissenters shall still receive as much here, though they deserve but little.

In a small treatise of the sufferings of the Episcopal clergy in Scotland, it will appear what usage they met with; how they not only lost their livings, but in several places were plundered and abused in their persons; the ministers that could not conform, turned out with numerous families, and no maintenance, and hardly charity enough left to relieve them with a bit of bread ; and the cruelties of the parties are innumerable, and not to be attempted in this short piece.

And now, to prevent the distant cloud which they perceived to hang over their heads from England, with a true Presbyterian policy, they put in for a union of nations, that England might unite their Church with the Kirk of Scotland, and their Presbyterian members sit in our House of Commons, and their assembly of Scotch canting long-cloaks in our Convocation. What might have been if our fanatic Whiggish statesmen continued, God only knows ; but we hope we are out of fear of that now.

It is alleged by some of the faction, and they began to bully us with it, that if we will not unite with them, they will not settle the Crown with us again, but when her Majesty dies will choose a king for themselves.

If they will not, we must make them, and it is not the first time we have let them know that we are able. The Crowns of these kingdoms have not so far disowned the right of succession but they may retrieve it again, and if Scotland thinks to come off from a successive to an elective state of government, England has not promised not to assist the right heirs, and put them into possession, without any regard to their ridiculous settlements.

These are the gentlemen, these their ways of treating the Church, both at home and abroad. Now let us examine the reasons they pretend to give why we should be favourable to them, why we should continue and tolerate them among us.

First, they are very numerous they say, they are a great part of the nation, and we cannot suppress them.

To this may be answered—1. They are not so numerous as the Protestants in France, and yet the French King effectually cleared the nation of them at once, and we do not find he misses them at home.

But I am not of the opinion they are so numerous as is pretended; their party is more numerous than their persons, and those mistaken people of the Church who are misled and deluded by their wheedling artifices to join with them, make their party the greater; but those will open their eyes when the Government shall set heartily about the work, and come off from them, as some animals, which, they say, always desert a house when it is likely to fall.

2. The more numerous the more dangerous, and therefore the more need to suppress them; and God has suffered us to bear them as goads in our sides, for not utterly extinguishing them long ago.

3. If we are to allow them only because we cannot suppress them, then it ought to be tried whether we can or no; and I am of opinion it is

easy to be done, and could prescribe ways and means, if it were proper; but I doubt not the Government will find effectual methods for the rooting the contagion from the face of this land.

Another argument they use, which is this, that it is a time of war, and we have need to unite against the common enemy.

We answer, this common enemy had been no enemy if they had not made him so; he was quiet, in peace, and no way disturbed or encroached upon us, and we know no reason we had to quarrel with him.

But further, we make no question but we are able to deal with this common enemy without their help; but why must we unite with them because of the enemy? Will they go over to the enemy if we do not prevent it by a union with them? We are very well contented they should, and make no question we shall be ready to deal with them and the common enemy too, and better without them than with them.

Besides, if we have a common enemy, there is the more need to be secure against our private enemies; if there is one common enemy, we have the less need to have an enemy in our bowels.

It was a great argument some people used against suppressing the old money, that it was a time of war, and it was too great a risk for the nation to run; if we should not master it, we should be undone; and yet the sequel proved the hazard was not so great but it might be mastered, and the success was answerable. The suppressing the Dissenters is not a harder work, nor a work of less necessity to the public: we can never enjoy a settled uninterrupted union and tranquillity in this nation till the spirit of Whiggism, faction, and schism is melted down like the old money.

To talk of the difficulty is to frighten ourselves with chimeras and notions of a powerful party, which are indeed a party without power; difficulties often appear greater at a distance than when they are searched into with judgment, and distinguished from the vapours and shadows that attend them.

We are not to be frightened with it; this age is wiser than that, by all our own experience, and theirs too. King Charles the First had early suppressed this party if he had taken more deliberate measures. In short, it is not worth arguing, to talk of their arms; their Monmouths, and Shaftesburys, and Argylls are gone; their Dutch Sanctuary is at an end; Heaven has made way for their destruction, and if we do not close with the divine occasion, we are to blame ourselves, and may remember that we had once an opportunity to serve the Church of England by extirpating her implacable enemies, and, having let slip the minute that Heaven presented, may experimentally complain, "Post est occasio calva."

Here are some popular objections in the way:

As first, the Queen has promised them to continue them in their tolerated liberty, and has told us she will be a religious observer of her word.

What her Majesty will do we cannot help, but what, as the head of the Church, she ought to do, is another case. Her Majesty has promised to protect and defend the Church of England, and if she cannot effectually do that without the destruction of the Dissenters, she must of course dispense with one promise to comply with another. But to answer this cavil more effectually: her Majesty did never promise to maintain the toleration to the destruction of the Church, but it is upon supposition that it may be compatible with the well-being and safety of the Church, which she had declared she would take especial care of. Now, if these two interests clash, it is plain her Majesty's intentions are to uphold, protect, defend, and establish the Church, and this we conceive is impossible.

Perhaps it may be said that the Church is in no immediate danger from the Dissenters, and therefore it is time enough; but this is a weak answer.

For first, if a danger be real, the distance of it is no argument against, but rather a spur to quicken us to prevention, lest it be too late hereafter.

And secondly, here is the opportunity, and the only one perhaps that ever the Church had, to secure herself and destroy her enemies.

The representatives of the nation have now an opportunity; the time is come which all good men have wished for, that the gentlemen of England may serve the Church of England, now they are protected and encouraged by a Church of England Queen.

"What will you do for your sister in the day that she shall be spoken for?"

If ever you will establish the best Christian Church in the world;

If ever you will suppress the spirit of enthusiasm;

If ever you will free the nation from the viperous brood that have so long sucked the blood of their mother;

If ever you will leave your posterity free from faction and rebellion, this is the time.

This is the time to pull up this heretical weed of sedition, that has so long disturbed the peace of our Church, and poisoned the good corn.

But, says another hot and cold objector, this is renewing fire and faggot, reviving the Act "De Heret. Comburendo;" this will be cruelty in its nature, and barbarous to all the world.

I answer, it is cruelty to kill a snake or a toad in cold blood, but the poison of their nature makes it a charity to our neighbours to destroy those creatures, not for any personal injury received, but for prevention; not for the evil they have done, but the evil they may do.

Serpents, toads, vipers, &c., are noxious to the body, and poison the sensitive life; these poison the soul, corrupt our posterity, ensnare our children, destroy the vitals of our happiness, our future felicity, and contaminate the whole mass.

Shall any law be given to such wild creatures? Some beasts are for sport, and the huntsmen give them advantages of ground; but some are knocked on the head by all possible ways of violence and surprise.

I do not prescribe fire and faggot, but, as Scipio said of Carthage, "Delenda est Carthago," they are to be rooted out of this nation, if ever we will live in peace, serve God, or enjoy our own. As for the manner, I leave it to those hands who have a right to execute God's justice on the nation's and the Church's enemies.

But if we must be frightened from this justice under the specious pretences, and odious sense of cruelty, nothing will be effected. It will be more barbarous to our own children and dear posterity, when they shall reproach their fathers, as we do ours, and tell us: "You had an opportunity to root out this cursed race from the world, under the favour and protection of a true English Queen, and out of your foolish pity you spared them, because, forsooth, you would not be cruel, and now our Church is suppressed and persecuted, our religion trampled under foot, our estates plundered, our persons imprisoned and dragged to gaols, gibbets, and scaffolds; your sparing this Amalekite race is our destruction, your mercy to them proves cruelty to your poor posterity."

How just will such reflections be, when our posterity shall fall under the merciless clutches of this uncharitable generation; when our Church shall be swallowed up in schism, faction, enthusiasm, and confusion; when our Government shall be devolved upon foreigners, and our monarchy dwindled into a republic.

It would be more rational for us, if we must spare this generation, to summon our own to a general massacre, and as we have brought them into the world free, send them out so, and not betray them to destruction by our supine negligence, and then cry it is mercy.

Moses was a merciful meek man, and yet with what fury did he run through the camp, and cut the throats of three-and-thirty thousand of his dear Israelites, that were fallen into idolatry; what was the reason? It was mercy to the rest to make these examples, to prevent the destruction of the whole army.

How many millions of future souls we save from infection and delusion if the present race of poisoned spirits were purged from the face of the land.

It is vain to trifle in this matter, the light foolish handling of them by mulcts, fines, &c.; it is their glory and their advantage. If the gallows instead of the counter, and the galleys instead of the fines, were the reward of going to a conventicle, to preach or hear, there would not be so many sufferers. The spirit of martyrdom is over; they that will go to church to be chosen sheriffs and mayors, would go to forty churches rather than be hanged.

If one severe law were made, and punctually executed, that whoever was found at a conventicle should be banished the nation, and the preacher be hanged, we should soon see an end of the tale. They would all come to church; and one age would make us all one again.

To talk of 5s. a month for not coming to the Sacrament, and 1s. per week for not coming to church, this is such a way of converting people as never was known; this is selling them a liberty to transgress for so much money. If it be not a crime, why do not we give them full licence? And if it be, no price ought to compound for the committing it, for that is selling a liberty to people to sin against God and the Government.

If it be a crime of the highest consequence, both against the peace and welfare of the nation, the glory of God, the good of the Church, and the happiness of the soul, let us rank it among capital offences, and let it receive a punishment in proportion to it.

We hang men for trifles, and banish them for

things not worth naming, but an offence against God and the Church, against the welfare of the world and the dignity of religion, shall be bought off for 5*s.*! This is such a shame to a Christian Government that it is with regret I transmit it to posterity.

If men sin against God, affront his ordinances, rebel against his Church, and disobey the precepts of their superiors, let them suffer as such capital crimes deserve; so will religion flourish, and this divided nation be once again united.

And yet the title of barbarous and cruel will soon be taken off from this law too. I am not supposing that all the Dissenters in England should be hanged or banished, but as in cases of rebellions and insurrections, if a few of the ringleaders suffer, the multitude are dismissed, so a few obstinate people being made examples, there is no doubt but the severity of the law would find a stop in the compliance of the multitude.

To make the reasonableness of this matter out of question, and more unanswerably plain, let us examine for what it is that this nation is divided into parties and factions, and let us see how they can justify a separation, or we of the Church of England can justify our bearing the insults and inconveniences of the party.

One of their leading pastors, and a man of as much learning as most among them, in his answer to a pamphlet, entitled "An Inquiry into the Occasional Conformity," hath these words (p. 27): "Do the religion of the Church and the meeting-houses make two religions? Wherein do they differ? The substance of the same religion is common to them both, and the modes and accidents are the things in which only they differ." P. 28: "Thirty-nine Articles are given us for the summary of our religion; thirty-six contain the substance of it, wherein we agree; three the additional Appendices, about which we have some differences."

Now if, as by their own acknowledgment, the Church of England is a true Church, and the difference between them is only in a few modes and accidents, why should we expect that they will suffer galleys, corporal punishment, and banishment for these trifles? There is no question but they will be wiser; even their own principles will not bear them out in it; they will certainly comply with the laws, and with reason; and though, at the first, severity may seem hard, the next age will feel nothing of it; the contagion will be rooted out; the disease being cured there will be no need of the operation; but, if they should venture to transgress, and fall into the pit, all the world must condemn their obstinacy, as being without ground from their own principles.

Thus the pretence of cruelty will be taken off, and the party actually suppressed, and the disquiets they have so often brought upon the nation prevented.

Their numbers and their wealth makes them haughty, and that it is so far from being an argument to persuade us to forbear them, that it is a warning to us, without any more delay, to reconcile them to the unity of the Church, or remove them from us.

At present, Heaven be praised, they are not so formidable as they have been, and it is our own fault if ever we suffer them to be so. Providence and the Church of England seems to join in this particular, that now the destroyers of the nation's peace may be overturned, and to this end the present opportunity seems to be put into our hands.

To this end her present Majesty seems reserved to enjoy the Crown, that the ecclesiastic as well as civil rights of the nation may be restored by her hand.

To this end the face of affairs have received such a turn in the process of a few months as never has been before; the leading men of the nation, the universal cry of the people, the unanimous request of the clergy, agree in this, that the deliverance of our Church is at hand.

For this end has Providence given such a Parliament, such a Convocation, such a gentry, and such a Queen as we never had before.

And what may be the consequences of a neglect of such opportunities? The succession of the Crown has but a dark prospect; another Dutch turn may make the hopes of it ridiculous and the practice impossible. Be the house of our future Princes never so well inclined, they will be foreigners, and many years will be spent in suiting the genius of strangers to this Crown and the interests of the nation; and how many ages it may be before the English Throne be filled with so much zeal and candour, so much tenderness and hearty affection to the Church, as we see it now covered with, who can imagine?

It is high time, then, for the friends of the Church of England to think of building up and establishing her in such a manner, that she may be no more invaded by foreigners, nor divided by factions, schisms, and error.

If this could be done by gentle and easy methods, I should be glad; but the wound is corroded, the vitals begin to mortify, and nothing but amputation of members can complete the cure; all the ways of tenderness and compassion, all persuasive arguments, have been made use of in vain.

The humour of the Dissenters has so increased among the people, that they hold the Church in defiance, and the house of God is an abomination among them: nay, they have brought up their posterity in such prepossessed aversions to our holy religion, that the ignorant mob think we are all idolaters and worshippers of Baal, and account it a sin to come within the walls of our churches.

The primitive Christians were not more shy of a heathen temple, or of meat offered to idols, nor the Jews of swine's flesh, than some of our Dissenters are of the Church, and the divine service solemnized therein.

This obstinacy must be rooted out with the profession of it; while the generation are left at liberty daily to affront God Almighty, and dishonour his holy worship, we are wanting in our duty to God and our mother the Church of England.

How can we answer it to God, to the Church, and to our posterity, to leave them entangled with fanaticism, error, and obstinacy, in the bowels of the nation; to leave them an enemy in their streets, that in time may involve them in the same crimes and endanger the utter extirpation of religion in the nation.

What is the difference betwixt this and being subjected to the power of the Church of Rome, from whence we have reformed? If one be an extreme on one hand, and one on another, it is equally destructive to the truth to have errors settled among us, let them be of what nature they will.

Both are enemies of our Church and of our peace, and why should it not be as criminal to admit an enthusiast as a Jesuit? Why should the Papist, with his seven sacraments, be worse than the Quaker with no sacraments at all? Why should religious houses be more intolerable than meeting-houses? Alas! the Church of England! What with Popery on one hand, and schismatics on the other, how has she been crucified between two thieves!

Now let us crucify the thieves. Let her foundations be established upon the destruction of her enemies, the doors of mercy being always open to the returning part of the deluded people; let the obstinate be ruled with the rod of iron.

Let all true sons of so holy and oppressed a mother, exasperated by her afflictions, harden their hearts against those who have oppressed her.

And may God Almighty put it into the hearts of all the friends of truth to lift up a standard against pride and Antichrist, that the posterity of the sons of error may be rooted out from the face of this land for ever.

THE CRISIS;

OR,

*A DISCOURSE REPRESENTING,
FROM THE MOST AUTHENTIC RECORDS, THE JUST
CAUSES OF THE LATE HAPPY REVOLUTION;*

AND

THE SEVERAL SETTLEMENTS
OF THE CROWNS OF ENGLAND AND SCOTLAND
ON HER MAJESTY; AND ON THE DEMISE OF HER MAJESTY
WITHOUT ISSUE, UPON THE MOST ILLUSTRIOUS PRINCESS SOPHIA,
ELECTRESS AND DUCHESS DOWAGER OF HANOVER, AND THE HEIRS OF
HER BODY BEING PROTESTANTS; BY PREVIOUS ACTS OF BOTH
PARLIAMENTS OF THE LATE KINGDOMS OF ENGLAND
AND SCOTLAND; AND CONFIRMED BY THE
PARLIAMENT OF GREAT BRITAIN.

WITH SOME SEASONABLE REMARKS ON THE
DANGER OF A POPISH SUCCESSOR.

Invitus ea tanquam vulnera attingo; sed nisi tacta tractataque sanari
non possunt.—LIV.

BY

RICHARD STEELE, Esq.

1714.

TO THE

CLERGY OF THE CHURCH OF ENGLAND.

GENTLEMEN,

It is with a just deference to your great power and influence in this kingdom, that I lay before you the following comment upon the laws which regard the settlement of the Imperial Crown of Great Britain. My purpose in addressing these matters to you, is to conjure you, as Heaven has blessed you with proper talents and opportunities, to recommend them, in your writings and discourses, to your fellow-subjects.

In the character of pastors and teachers, you have an almost irresistible power over us of your congregations; and by the admirable institution of our laws, the tenths of our lands, now in your possession, are destined to become the property of such others as shall by learning and virtue qualify themselves to succeed you. These circumstances of education and fortune place the minds of the people, from age to age, under your direction. As, therefore, it would be the highest indiscretion in

Ministers of State of this kingdom to neglect the care of being acceptable to you in their administration, so it would be the greatest impiety in you to inflame the people committed to your charge with apprehensions of danger to you and your constitution, from men innocent of any such designs.

Give me leave, who have in all my words and actions, from my youth upwards, maintained an inviolable respect to you and your order, to observe to you that all the dissatisfactions which have been raised in the minds of the people owe their rise to the cunning of artful men, who have introduced the mention of you and your interest, which are sacred to all good men, to cover and sanctify their own practices upon the affections of the people, for ends very different from the promotion of religion and virtue. Give me leave also to take notice that these suggestions have been favoured by some few unwary men in holy orders, who have made the constitution of their own country a very little part of their study, and yet made obedience and government the frequent subjects of their discourses.

These men, from the pompous ideas of imperial greatness, and submission to absolute emperors, which they imbibed in their earlier years, have from time to time inadvertently uttered notions of power and obedience abhorrent from the laws of this their native country.

I will take the further liberty to say, that if the

Acts of Parliament mentioned in the following treatise had been from time to time put in a fair and clear light, and been carefully recommended to the perusal of young gentlemen in colleges, with a preference to all other civil institutions whatsoever, this kingdom had not been in its present condition, but the constitution would have had, in every member the universities have sent into the world ever since the Revolution, an advocate for our rights and liberties.

There is one thing which deserves your most serious consideration. You have bound yourselves, by the strongest engagements that religion can lay upon men, to support that succession which is the subject of the following papers; you have tied down your souls by an oath to maintain it as it is settled in the House of Hanover; nay, you have gone much further than is usual in cases of this nature, as you have personally abjured the Pretender to this Crown, and that expressly, without any equivocations or mental reservations whatsoever, that is, without any possible escapes, by which the subtlety of temporizing casuists might hope to elude the force of these solemn obligations. You know much better than I do, whether the calling God to witness to the sincerity of our intentions in these cases, whether the swearing upon the holy Evangelists in the most solemn manner, whether the taking of an oath before multitudes of fellow-subjects and fellow-Christians in our public courts of justice, do not lay the greatest obligations that can be laid on the consciences of men. This I am sure of, that if the body of a clergy who considerately and voluntarily entered into these engagements should be made use of as instruments and examples to make the nation break through them, not only the succession to our Crown, but the very essence of our religion, is in danger. What a triumph would it furnish to those evil men among us who are enemies to your sacred order? What occasion would it administer to atheists and unbelievers, to say that Christianity is nothing else but an outward show and pretence among the most knowing of its professors? What could we afterwards object to Jesuits? What would be the scandal brought upon our holy Church, which is at present the glory and bulwark of the Reformation? How would our present clergy appear in the eyes of their posterity, and even to the successors of their own order, under a Government introduced and established by a conduct so directly opposite to all the rules of honour and precepts of Christianity?

As I always speak and think of your holy order with the utmost deference and respect, I do not insist upon this subject to insinuate that there is such a disposition among your venerable body, but to show how much your own honour and the interest of religion is concerned that there should be no cause given for it.

Under colour of a zeal towards you, men may sometimes act not only with impunity, but popularity, what would render them, without that hypocrisy, insufferably odious to their fellow-subjects.

Under this pretence men may presume to practise such arts for the destruction and dishonour of their country as it would be impious to make use of even for its glory and safety: men may do in the highest prosperity what it would not be excusable to attempt under the lowest necessity!

The laws of our country, the powers of the legislature, the faith of nations, and the honour of God may be too weak considerations to bear up against the popular though groundless cry of the Church. This fatal prepossession may shelter men in raising the French name and Roman Catholic interest in Great Britain, and consequently in all Europe.

It behoves you therefore, gentlemen, to consider whether the cry of the Church's danger may not at length become a truth; and, as you are men of sense and men of honour, to exert yourselves in undeceiving the multitude, whenever their affectionate concern for you may prove fatal to themselves.

You are surrounded by a learned, wealthy, and knowing gentry, who can distinguish your merit, and do honour to your characters. They know with what firmness as Englishmen, with what self-denial as prelates, with what charity as Christians, the Lords the Bishops, fathers of the Church, have behaved themselves in the public cause; they know what contumelies the rest of the clergy have undergone, what discountenance they have laboured under, what prejudice they have suffered in their ministry, who have adhered to the cause of truth; but it is certain that the face of things is now too melancholy to bear any longer false appearances; and common danger has united men, who not long ago were artfully inflamed against each other, into some regard of their common safety.

When the world is in this temper, those of our pastors, whose exemplary lives and charitable dispositions both adorn and advance our holy religion, will be the objects of our love and admiration; and those who pursue the gratifications of pride, ambition and avarice, under the sacred character of clergymen, will not fail to be our contempt and derision.

Noise and wrath cannot always pass for zeal; and if we see but little of the public spirit of Englishmen or the charity of Christians in others, it is certain we can feel but little of the pleasure of love and gratitude, and but faint emotions of respect and veneration in ourselves.

It will be an action worthy the ministers of the Church of England to distinguish themselves for the love of their country; and, as we have a religion that wants no assistance from artifice or enlargement of secular power, but is well supported by the wisdom and piety of its preachers, and its own native truth, to let mankind see that we have a clergy who are of the people, obedient to the same laws, and zealous not only of the supremacy and prerogative of our princes, but of the liberties of their fellow-subjects: this will make us who are your flock burn with joy to see, and with zeal to imitate, your lives and actions. It cannot be expected but that there will be, in so great a body, light, superficial, vain, and ambitious men, who, being untouched with the sublime force of the Gospel, will think it their interest to insinuate jealousies between the clergy and laity, in hopes to derive from their order a veneration which they know they cannot deserve from their virtue. But while the most worthy, conspicuous, learned, and powerful of your sacred function are moved by the noble and generous incentives of doing good to the souls of men, we will not doubt of seeing by your ministry the love of our country, due regard for our laws and liberties, and resentment for the abuse of truth revive in the hearts of men. And as there are no instruments under heaven so capable of this great work, that God would make you such to this divided nation is the hearty prayer of,

    Gentlemen,
  Your most dutiful and most obedient
    humble servant,
     RICHARD STEELE.

PREFACE.

I NEVER saw an unruly crowd of people cool by degrees into temper, but it gave me an idea of the original of power and the nature of civil institutions. One particular man has usually in those cases, from the dignity of his appearance, or other qualities known or imagined by the multitude, been received into sudden favour and authority; the occasion of their difference has been represented to him, and the matter referred to his decision.

This first step towards acting reasonably has brought them to themselves; and when the person, by an appeal to whom they first were taken out of confusion, was gone from amongst them, they have calmly taken further measures from a sense of their common good.

Absolute unlimited power in one person seems to have been the first and natural recourse of mankind from disorder and rapine, and such a government must be acknowledged to be better than no government at all; but all restrictions of power made by laws and participation of sovereignty among several persons are apparent improvements made upon what began in that unlimited power. This is what seems reasonable to common sense, and the manner of maintaining absolute dominion in one person, wherever it subsists, verifies the observation; for the subjection of the people to such authority is supported only by terrors, sudden and private executions and imprisonments, and not, as with happy Britons, by the judgment, in cases of liberty and property, of the peers and neighbours of men accused or prosecuted. This absolute power in one person as it is generally exercised is not indeed government, but at best clandestine tyranny, supported by the confederates, or rather favourite slaves, of the tyrant.

I was glad to find this natural sense of power confirmed in me by very great and good men, who have made government, and the principles on which it is founded, their professed study and meditation.

A very celebrated author has these words :—

"The case of man's nature standing as it does, some kind of regiment the law of nature doth require; yet the kinds thereof being many, nature tieth not to any one, but leaveth the choice as a thing arbitrary. At the first, when some certain kind of regiment was once approved, it may be that nothing was then further thought upon for the manner of governing, but all permitted unto their wisdom and discretion which were to rule, till by experience they found this for all parts very inconvenient, so as the thing which they had devised for a remedy did indeed but increase the sore which it should have cured. They saw that to live by one man's will became the cause of all men's misery. This constrained them to come unto laws, wherein all men might see their duties beforehand, and know the penalties of transgressing them. Men always knew that when force and injury was offered, they might be defenders of themselves; they knew that, howsoever men might seek their own commodity, yet if this were done with injury to others it was not to be suffered, but by all men and by all good means to be withstood.

"Finally, they knew that no man might in reason take upon him to determine his own right, and according to his own determination proceed in maintenance thereof, inasmuch as every man is towards himself, and them whom he greatly affecteth, partial; and therefore that strifes and troubles would be endless, except they have their common consent all to be ordered by some whom they should agree upon."

Mr Stanhope, in defence of resistance in cases of extreme necessity, cites this memorable passage from Grotius :—

"If the king hath one part of the supreme power, and the other part is in the senate or people, when such a king shall invade that part that doth not belong to him, it shall be lawful to oppose a just force to him, because his power does not extend so far; which position I hold to be true, even though the power of making war should be vested only in the king, which must be understood to relate only to foreign war; for, as for home, it is impossible for any to have a share of the supreme power and not to have likewise a right to defend that share."

An eminent divine, who deserves all honour for the obligations he has laid upon both Church and State by his writings on the subject of government, argues against unlimited power thus:—

"The question is, whether the power of the civil magistrate be unlimited—that is, in other words, whether the nature of his office require it to be so. But what? Is it the end of that office that one particular person may do what he pleaseth without restraint, or that society should be made happy and secure? Who will say the former? And if the latter be the true end of it, a less power than absolute will answer it—nay, an absolute power is a power to destroy that end, and therefore inconsistent with the end itself."

These passages I thought fit to produce by way of preface to the following discourse, as carrying in them the reason and foundation of government itself and in maintenance of what passed at the Revolution.

I shall only beg leave to add to them one very great living authority, the present Lord High Chancellor of Great Britain, who, in a late famous trial, did openly, before Queen, Lords, and Commons, maintain the lawfulness of the Revolution under the notion of resistance, and assert, before the most solemn and august assembly of Europe, that there are extraordinary cases, cases of necessity, which are implied, though not expressed, in the general rule—that is, which are so plain and so open to the common sense of mankind that, even whilst you are declaring resistance in all cases to be unlawful, you are of necessity understood to mean that resistance in some cases is lawful. I am pleased to observe, that no one ever put the matter so strongly, or carried it so high as this great man did upon that critical occasion. At the same time he was so just to his country as to declare that such a case undoubtedly the Revolution was, when our late unhappy sovereign then upon the throne, misled by evil counsellors, endeavoured to subvert and extirpate the Protestant religion and the laws and liberties of the kingdom.

THE CRISIS.

IT is every man's duty to correct the extravagances of his will, in order to enjoy life as becomes a rational being; but we cannot possess our souls with pleasure and satisfaction except we preserve to ourselves that inestimable blessing which we call liberty. By liberty I desire to be understood to mean the happiness of men's living under laws of their own making, by their personal consent or that of their representatives.

Without this the distinctions amongst mankind are but gentler degrees of misery; for as the true life of man consists in conducting it according to his own just sentiments and innocent inclinations, his being is degraded below that of a free agent, which Heaven has made him, when his affections and passions are no longer governed by the dictates of his own mind and the interests of human society, but by the arbitrary unrestrained will of another.

Without liberty, even health and strength, and all the advantages bestowed on us by Nature and Providence, may, at the will of a tyrant, be employed to our own ruin, and that of our fellow-creatures.

Liberty is essential to our happiness, and they who resign life itself rather than part with it do only a prudent action; but those who lay it down, and voluntarily expose themselves to death in behalf of their friends and country, do an heroic one. The more exalted part of our species are moved by such generous impulses as these; but even the community, the mass of mankind, when convinced of the danger of their civil rights, are anxious of preserving to themselves that dearest of all possessions, liberty.

The late kingdoms of England and Scotland have contended for it from age to age with too great a price of blood and treasure to be given for the purchase of any other blessing, but laid out parsimoniously when we consider they have transmitted this to their posterity.

But since, by I know not what fatality, we are of late grown supine, and our anxiety for it is abated, in proportion to the danger to which it is every day more exposed by the artful and open attacks of the enemies of our Constitution, it is a seasonable and honest office to look into our circumstances, and let the enemies of our present establishment behold the securities which the laws of our country have given those who dare assert their liberties, and the terrors which they have pronounced against those who dare undermine them. For, whatever is the prospect before our eyes, it is the business of every honest man to look up with a spirit that becomes honesty, and to do what in him lies for the improvement of our present condition, which nothing but our own pusillanimity can make desperate.

The most destructive circumstance in our affairs seems to be that, by the long and repeated insinuations of our enemies, many are worn into a kind of doubt of their own cause, and think with patience of what is suggested in favour of contrary pretensions. The most obvious method of reviving the proper sentiments in the minds of men for what they ought to esteem most dear, is to show that our cause has in it all the sanctions of honour, truth, and justice, and that we are, by all the laws of God and man, instated in a condition of enjoying religion, life, liberty, and property, rescued from the most imminent danger of having them all for ever depend upon the arbitrary power of a Popish prince.

We should have been chained down in this abject condition in the reign of the late King James, had not God Almighty in mercy given us the late happy Revolution, by that glorious instrument of his providence the great and memorable King William. But though this wonderful deliverance happened as it were but yesterday, yet such is the inadvertency or ingratitude of some amongst us, that they seem not only to have forgotten the deliverer, but even the deliverance itself. Old men act as if they believed the danger which then hung over their heads was only a dream, the wild effects of ill-grounded imaginary fears; and young men, as if they had never heard from their fathers, nor read of what passed in this kingdom, at a period no farther backward than the space of five-and-twenty years.

I flatter myself that if the passages which happened in those days, the resolutions of the nation thereupon, and the just provisions made from time to time against our falling into the same disasters, were fairly stated and laid in one view, all indirect arts and mean subtleties practised to weaken our securities would be frustrated, and vanish before the glaring light of law and reason.

I shall not govern myself on this occasion by the partial relation of particular persons or parties, but by the sense of the whole people, by the sense of the Houses of Lords and Commons, the representative body of the whole nation, in whose resolutions, according to the different state of things, the condition of the kingdom, by those who had the greatest stakes in it, has been from time to time plainly, impartially, and pathetically expressed.

I shall begin with the Act of Parliament made in England in the second session of the first year of the late King William and Queen Mary, intituled "An Act declaring the Rights and Liberties of the Subject, and settling the Succession of the Crown."

It carries in it the noble resentment of a people that had been just rescued from tyranny; and yet, that they might justify their actions to posterity, it recites all the particular instances of the tyrannical reign in a plain and dispassionate simplicity. The Act runs as follows:—

"Whereas, the Lords Spiritual and Temporal, and Commons, assembled at Westminster, lawfully, fully, and freely representing all the estates of the people of this realm, did upon the 13th day of February, in the year of our Lord 1688, present unto their Majesties, then called and known by the names and style of William and Mary, Prince and Princess of Orange, being present in their proper persons, a certain declaration in writing, made by the said Lords and Commons in the words following, viz.:—

"Whereas the late King James the Second, by the assistance of divers evil Counsellors, Judges, and Ministers employed by him, did endeavour to subvert and extirpate the Protestant religion and the laws and liberties of this kingdom;

"By assuming and exercising a power of dispensing with and suspending of laws and the execution of laws, without consent of Parliament;

"By committing and prosecuting divers worthy prelates, for humbly petitioning to be excused from concurring to the said assumed power;

"By issuing, and causing to be executed, a Commission under the Great Seal for erecting a court called the Court of Commissioners for Ecclesiastical Causes;

"By levying money for and to the use of the Crown, by pretence of prerogative, for other time and in other manner than the same was granted by Parliament;

"By raising and keeping a standing army within this kingdom in time of peace without consent of Parliament, and quartering soldiers contrary to law;

"By causing several good subjects, being Protestants, to be disarmed, at the same time when Papists were both armed and employed, contrary to law;

"By violating the freedom of election of members to serve in Parliament;

"By prosecutions in the Court of King's Bench for matters and causes cognizable only in Parliament, and by divers other arbitrary and illegal courses:

"And whereas of late years partial, corrupt and unqualified persons have been returned and served on juries, in trials, and particularly divers jurors in trials for high treason which were not freeholders;

"And excessive bail hath been required of persons committed in criminal cases, to elude the benefit of the laws made for the liberty of the subjects;

"And excessive fines have been imposed,

"And illegal and cruel punishments inflicted,

"And several grants and promises made of fines and forfeitures, before any conviction or judgment against the persons upon whom the same were to be levied;

"All which are utterly and directly contrary to the known laws and statutes and freedom of this realm:

"And whereas the said late King James the Second having abdicated the government, and the throne being thereby vacant,

"His Highness the Prince of Orange (whom it hath pleased Almighty God to make the glorious instrument of delivering this kingdom from Popery and arbitrary power) did (by the advice of the Lords Spiritual and Temporal, and divers principal persons of the Commons) cause letters to be written to the Lords Spiritual and Temporal, being Protestants, and other letters to the several counties, cities, universities, boroughs, and Cinque ports, for the choosing of such persons to represent them as were of right to be sent to Parliament, to meet and sit at Westminster upon the two and twentieth day of January, in this year one thousand six hundred eighty and eight, in order to such an establishment, as that their religion, laws, and liberties might not again be in danger of being subverted, upon which letters elections having been accordingly made;

"And thereupon the said Lords Spiritual and Temporal, and Commons, pursuant to their respective letters and elections, being now assembled in a full and free representative of this nation, taking into their most serious consideration the best means for attaining the ends aforesaid, do, in the first place, as their ancestors in like case have usually done, for the vindicating and asserting their ancient rights and liberties, declare:

"That the pretended power of suspending of laws or the execution of laws by regal authority, without consent of Parliament, is illegal;

"That the pretended power of dispensing with laws or the execution of laws by regal authority, as it hath been assumed and exercised of late, is illegal;

"That the Commission for erecting the late Court of Commissioners for Ecclesiastical Causes, and all other commissions and courts of like nature, are illegal and pernicious;

"That levying money for or to the use of the Crown, by pretence of prerogative, without grant of Parliament, for longer time or in other manner than the same is or shall be granted, is illegal;

"That it is the right of the subjects to petition the King, and all commitments and prosecutions for such petitioning are illegal;

"That the raising or keeping a standing army within the kingdom in time of peace, unless it be with consent of Parliament, is against law;

"That the subjects which are Protestants may have arms for their defence suitable to their conditions, and as allowed by law;

"That elections of members ought to be free;

"That the freedom of speech and debates, or proceedings in Parliament, ought not to be impeached or questioned in any court or place out of Parliament;

"That excessive bail ought not to be required, nor excessive fines imposed, nor cruel and unusual punishments inflicted;

"That jurors ought to be duly impanelled and returned, and jurors which pass upon men in trials for high treason ought to be freeholders;

"That all grants, and promises of fines, and forfeitures of particular persons before conviction, are illegal and void;

"And that for redress of all grievances, and for the amending, strengthening, and preserving of the laws, Parliaments ought to be held frequently;

"And they do claim, demand, and insist upon all and singular the premises, as their undoubted rights and liberties; and that no declarations, judgments, doings, or proceedings to the prejudice of the people in any of the said premises ought in any wise to be drawn hereafter into consequence or example.

"To which demand of their rights they are particularly encouraged by the declaration of his Highness the Prince of Orange, as being the only means for obtaining a full redress and remedy therein;

"Having therefore an entire confidence that his said Highness the Prince of Orange will perfect the deliverance so far advanced by him, and will still preserve them from the violation of their rights which they have here asserted, and from all other attempts upon their religion, rights, and liberties;

"The said Lords Spiritual and Temporal, and Commons, assembled at Westminster, do resolve:

"That William and Mary, Prince and Princess of Orange, be and be declared King and Queen of England, France, and Ireland, and the dominions thereunto belonging; to hold the Crown and royal dignity of the said kingdoms and dominions, to them the said Prince and Princess during their lives, and the life of the survivor of them; and that the sole and full exercise of the regal power be only in and executed by the said Prince of Orange in the names of the said Prince and Princess during their joint lives, and after their deceases the said crown and royal dignity of the said kingdoms and dominions to be to the heirs of the body of the said Princess, and, for default of such issue, to the Princess Anne of Denmark and the heirs of her body; and, for default of such issue, to the heirs of the body of the said Prince of Orange.

"And the Lords Spiritual and Temporal, and Commons, do pray the said Prince and Princess to accept the same accordingly.

"And that the oaths hereafter mentioned be taken by all persons, of whom the oaths of allegiance and supremacy might be required by law, instead of them; and that the said oaths of allegiance and supremacy be abrogated.

"'I, A. B. do sincerely promise and swear that I will be faithful and bear true allegiance to their Majesties King William and Queen Mary. So help me God.

"'I, A. B. do swear that I do from my heart abhor, detest, and abjure, as impious and heretical, this damnable doctrine and position, that princes excommunicated or deprived by the Pope, or any authority of the See of Rome, may be deposed or murdered by their subjects, or any other whatsoever.

"'And I do declare that no foreign prince, person, prelate, state, or potentate hath, or ought to have, any jurisdiction, power, superiority, pre-eminence or authority, ecclesiastical or spiritual, within this realm. So help me God.'

"Upon which their said Majesties did accept the Crown and royal dignity of the kingdoms of England, France, and Ireland, and the dominions thereunto belonging, according to the resolution and desire of the said Lords and Commons contained in the said declaration.

"And thereupon their Majesties were pleased that the said Lords Spiritual and Temporal, and Commons, being the two Houses of Parliament, should continue to sit, and, with their Majesties' royal concurrence, make effectual provision for the settlement of the religion, laws, and liberties of this kingdom; so that the same for the future might not be in danger again of being subverted; to which the said Lords Spiritual and Temporal, and Commons, did agree, and proceed to act accordingly.

"Now in pursuance of the premises, the said Lords Spiritual and Temporal, and Commons, in Parliament assembled, for the ratifying, confirming, and establishing the said declaration, and the articles, clauses, matters, and things therein contained by the force of a law made in due form by authority of Parliament, do pray that it may be declared and enacted, that all and singular the rights and liberties asserted and claimed in the said declaration are the true, ancient, and indubitable rights and liberties of the people of this kingdom, and so shall be esteemed, allowed, adjudged, deemed, and taken to be; and that all and every the particulars aforesaid shall be firmly and strictly holden and observed, as they are expressed in the said declaration; and all officers and ministers whatsoever shall serve their Majesties and their successors according to the same in all times to come.

"And the said Lords Spiritual and Temporal, and Commons, seriously considering how it hath pleased Almighty God, in his marvellous providence and merciful goodness to this nation, to provide and preserve their said Majesties' royal persons most happily to reign over us upon the throne of their ancestors, for which they render unto Him from the bottom of their hearts their humblest thanks and praises, do truly, firmly, assuredly, and in the sincerity of their hearts think, and do hereby recognize, acknowledge, and declare, that King James the Second having abdicated the government, and their Majesties having accepted the Crown and royal dignity as aforesaid, their said Majesties did become, were, are, and of right ought to be by the laws of this realm, our Sovereign Liege Lord and Lady King and Queen of England, France, and Ireland, and the dominions thereunto belonging, in and to whose princely persons the royal state, crown, and dignity of the said realms, with all honours, styles, titles, regalities, prerogatives, powers, jurisdictions, and authorities to the same belonging and appertaining, are most fully, rightfully, and entirely invested and incorporated, united and annexed.

"And for preventing all questions and divisions in this realm, by reason of any pretended titles to the Crown, and for preserving a certainty in the succession thereof, in and upon which the unity, peace, tranquillity, and safety of this nation doth, under God, wholly consist and depend ;

"The said Lords Spiritual and Temporal, and Commons, do beseech their Majesties, that it may be enacted, established, and declared that the Crown and regal government of the said kingdoms and dominions, with all and singular the premises thereunto belonging and appertaining, shall be and continue to their said Majesties, and the survivor of them, during their lives, and the life of the survivor of them; and that the entire, perfect, and full exercise of the regal power and government be only in and executed by his Majesty, in the names of both their Majesties during their joint lives ; and after their deceases, the said Crown and premises shall be and remain to the heirs of the body of her Majesty ; and, for default of such issue, to her Royal Highness the Princess Anne of Denmark, and the heirs of her body ; and, for default of such issue, to the heirs of the body of his said Majesty. And thereunto the said Lords Spiritual and Temporal, and Commons, do, in the name of all the people aforesaid, most humbly and faithfully submit themselves, their heirs and posterities for ever ; and do faithfully promise that they will stand to, maintain, and defend their said Majesties, and also the limitation and succession of the Crown herein specified and contained, to the utmost of their powers, with their lives and estates, against all persons whatsoever that shall attempt anything to the contrary.

"And whereas it hath been found by experience that it is inconsistent with the safety and welfare of this Protestant kingdom to be governed by a Popish prince, or by any King or Queen marrying a Papist;

"The said Lords Spiritual and Temporal, and Commons, do further pray that it may be enacted that all and every person and persons that is, are, or shall be reconciled to, or shall hold communion with the See or Church of Rome, or shall profess the Popish religion, or shall marry a Papist, shall be excluded, and be for ever incapable to inherit, possess, or enjoy the Crown and government of this realm, and Ireland, and the dominions thereunto belonging, or any part of the same; or to have, use, or exercise any regal power, authority, or jurisdiction within the same; and in all, and every such case, or cases, the people of these realms shall be, and are hereby absolved of their allegiance; and the said Crown and government shall from time to time descend to and be enjoyed by such person or persons, being Protestants, as should have inherited and enjoyed the same, in case the said person or persons so reconciled, holding communion, or professing or marrying as aforesaid, were naturally dead.

"And that every King and Queen of this realm, who any time hereafter shall come to and succeed in the Imperial Crown of this kingdom, shall, on the first day of the meeting of the first Parliament next after his or her coming to the Crown, sitting in his or her throne in the House of Peers, in the presence of the Lords and Commons therein assembled, or at his or her coronation, before such person or persons who shall administer the coronation oath to him or her, at the time of his or her taking the said oath (which shall first happen), make, subscribe, and audibly repeat the declaration mentioned in the statute made in the thirtieth year of the reign of King Charles the Second, entitled 'An Act for the more effectual preserving the King's person and government, by disabling Papists from sitting in either House of Parliament.' But if it shall happen that such King or Queen, upon his or her succession to the Crown of this realm, shall be under the age of twelve years, then every such King or Queen shall make, subscribe, and audibly repeat the said declaration at his or her coronation, or the first day of the meeting of the first Parliament as aforesaid which shall first happen after such King or Queen shall have attained the said age of twelve years.

"All which their Majesties are contented and pleased shall be declared, enacted, and established, by authority of this present Parliament, and shall stand, remain, and be the law of this realm for ever; and the same are by their said Majesties, by and with the advice and consent of the Lords Spiritual and Temporal, and Commons in Parliament assembled, and by the authority of the same, declared, enacted, and established accordingly.

"And be it further declared and enacted by the authority aforesaid, that, from and after this present session of Parliament, no dispensation by 'Non obstante,' of or to any statute, or part thereof, shall be allowed, but that the same shall be held void and of no effect, except a dispensation be allowed of in such statute, and except in such cases as shall be especially provided for by one or more Bill or Bills, to be passed during the present session of Parliament.

"Provided that no charter, or grant, or pardon, granted before the three and twentieth day of October, in the year of our Lord 1689, shall be any ways impeached or invalidated by this Act, but that the same shall be and remain of the same force and effect in law, and no other, than as if this Act had never been made."

I have recited the Act at large, that I might on the one hand show the just sense the English nation then had of their deliverance, and their gratitude to their deliverer the glorious King William; and, on the other hand, avoid being censured for heaping more miscarriages upon that unhappy prince King

James, than a nation, whose religion, liberties, fortunes, and lives were just snatched from the brink of ruin thought fit to charge him with. And here, that I may do justice to the Scots nation as well as to the English, I shall also set down, as succinctly as I can, what that brave people did in this important juncture.

The Convention of the Lords and Commons in the beginning of the year 1689 came to the resolutions in substance as follow, viz.:—

"That whereas King James the Seventh, being a professed Papist, did assume the royal power, and act as King, without ever taking the oath required by law, whereby every King at his accession to the government was obliged to swear to maintain the Protestant religion, and to rule the people according to the laudable laws; and, by the advice of wicked counsellors, did invade the fundamental constitution of the kingdom of Scotland, and altered it from a legal limited monarchy to an arbitrary and despotic power; and in a public proclamation asserted an absolute power to annul and disable all laws, particularly by arraigning the laws establishing the Protestant religion, and exerted that power to the subversion of the Protestant religion, and to the violation of the laws and liberties of the kingdom.

"By erecting public schools and societies of the Jesuits, and not only allowing Mass to be publicly said, but also converting Protestant chapels and churches to public Mass houses, contrary to the express laws against saying and hearing Mass;

"By allowing Popish books to be printed and dispersed by a patent to a Popish printer, designing him printer to his Majesty's household, college, and chapel, contrary to law;

"By taking the children of Protestant noblemen and gentlemen, sending them abroad to be bred Papists, and bestowing pensions upon priests to pervert Protestants from their religion by offers of places and preferments;

"By discharging Protestants, at the same time he employed Papists in places of greatest trust both civil and military, &c., and entrusting the forts and magazines in their hands;

"By imposing oaths contrary to law;

"By exacting money without consent of Parliament or Convention of Estates;

"By levying and keeping up a standing army in time of peace, without consent of Parliament, and maintaining them upon free quarter;

"By employing the officers of the army as judges throughout the kingdom, by whom the subjects were put to death without legal trial, jury, or record;

"By imposing exorbitant fines to the value of the parties' estates, exacting extravagant bail, and disposing fines and forfeitures before any process or conviction;

"By imprisoning persons without expressing the reason, and delaying to bring them to trial;

"By causing several persons to be prosecuted, and their estates to be forfeited, upon stretches of old and obsolete laws, upon weak and frivolous pretences, and upon lame and defective proofs; as particularly the late Earl of Argyle, to the scandal of the justice of the nation;

"By subverting the rights of the royal boroughs, the third estate of Parliament, imposing upon them not only magistrates, but also the whole town council and clerks, contrary to their liberties and express charters, without any pretence of sentence, surrender, or consent; so that the commisioners to Parliament being chosen by the magistrates and councils, the King might in effect as well nominate the estate of Parliament. Besides that, many of the magistrates by him put in were Papists, and the boroughs were forced to pay money for the letters imposing those illegal magistrates upon them;

"By sending letters to the chief courts of justice, not only ordering the judges to stop 'sine die,' but also commanding how to proceed in cases depending before them, contrary to the express laws; and by changing the nature of the judges' patents 'ad vitam' or 'culpam,' into a commission 'de bene placito,' to dispose them to a compliance with arbitrary courses, and turning them out of their offices if they refused to comply;

"By granting personal protections for civil debts contrary to law;

"All which miscarriages of King James were utterly and directly contrary to the known laws, freedoms, and statutes of the realm of Scotland. Upon which grounds and reasons the estates of the kingdom of Scotland did find and declare that the said King James had forfeited the Crown, and the throne was become vacant.

"Therefore in regard his Royal Highness, then Prince of Orange, since King of England, whom it hath pleased God to make the glorious instrument of delivering these kingdoms from Popery and arbitrary power, by advice of several lords and gentlemen of the Scots nation then at London, did call the Estates of this kingdom to meet upon the 14th of March last, in order to such an establishment as that the religion, laws, and liberties might not again be in danger of being subverted; the said estates being then assembled accordingly, in a full and free representative of the nation, did in the first place, as their ancestors in like cases had usually done for vindicating and asserting their ancient rights and liberties, declare:

"That by the law of Scotland no Papist could be King or Queen of the realm, nor bear any office therein; nor that any Protestant successor could exercise the regal power till they have sworn the coronation oath.

"That all proclamations asserting an absolute power to null and disable laws, in order for erecting schools and colleges for Jesuits, converting Protestant churches and chapels into Mass houses, and the allowing Mass to be said, and the allowing Popish books to be printed and dispersed, was contrary to law.

"That the taking the children of noblemen, gentlemen, and others, and keeping them abroad to be bred papists;

"The making funds and donations to Popish schools and colleges, the bestowing pensions on priests, and the seducing Protestants from their religion by offers of places and preferments, was contrary to law.

"That the disarming of Protestants, and employing Papists in the greatest places of trust, both civil and military, was contrary to law.

"That the imposing an oath without authority of Parliament was contrary to law.

"That the raising of money without consent of Parliament or Convention was contrary to law.

"That employing the officers of the army as judges was contrary to law.

"That the imposing extraordinary fines, &c., was contrary to law.

"That the imprisoning of persons without expressing the reasons was contrary to law.

"That the prosecuting, and seizing men's estates

as forfeited upon stretches of old and obsolete laws, &c., was contrary to law.

"That the nominating and imposing magistrates, &c., upon boroughs, contrary to their express charters, was contrary to law.

"That the sending letters to the courts of justice, ordering the judges to desist from determining of causes, and ordering them how to proceed in causes depending before them, &c., was contrary to law.

"That the granting of personal protections, &c., was contrary to law.

"That the forcing the subjects to depose against themselves in capital causes, however the punishments were restricted, was contrary to law.

"That the using torture without evidence, or in ordinary crimes, was contrary to law.

"That the sending of an army in a warlike manner into any part of the kingdom in time of peace, and exacting locality and free quarters, was contrary to law.

"That the charging the subjects with law boroughs at the King's instance, and imposing bonds without authority of Parliament, and the suspending advocates for not appearing when bonds were offered, was contrary to law.

"That the putting garrisons into private houses in time of peace, without authority of Parliament, was illegal.

"That the opinions of the Lords of the Session in

the two cases following, were illegal, (viz.): That the concerting the demand of the supply of a fore faulted person, although not given, was treason; and that persons refusing to discover their private thoughts in relation to points of treason, or other men's actions, are guilty of treason.

"That the fining husbands for their wives' withdrawing from Church was illegal.

"That prelacy and superiority of an office in the Church above Presbyters is and has been a great and insupportable burden to this nation, and contrary to the inclinations of the generality of the people ever since the Reformation, they having reformed Popery by Presbytery, and therefore ought to be abolished.

"That it is the right and privilege of the subject to protest for remedy of law to the King and Parliament, against sentences pronounced by the Lords of the Sessions, provided the same do not stop executions of the said sentences.

"That it is the right of the subject to petition the King, and that all prosecutions and imprisonments for such petitioning were contrary to law.

"Therefore for the redress of all grievances, and for the amending, strengthening, and preserving the laws, they claimed that Parliaments ought to be frequently called, and allowed to sit, and freedom of speech and debate allowed the members; and further claimed and insisted upon all and sundry the premises, as their undoubted rights and liberties ; and that no declaration or proceedings to the prejudice of the people, in any the said premises, ought in any wise to be drawn hereafter in example ; but that all forfeitures, fines, loss of offices, imprisonments, banishments, prosecutions, and rigorous executions be considered, and the parties redressed.

"To which demand of their rights, and redress of their grievances, they took themselves to be encouraged by the King of England's declaration for the kingdom of Scotland, in October last, as being the only means for obtaining a full redress and remedy therein.

"Therefore for as much as they had an entire confidence that his Majesty of England would perfect the deliverance so far advanced by him, and would still preserve them from the violation of the rights which they had asserted, and from all other attempts upon their religion, laws, and liberties ;

"The estates of the kingdom of Scotland had resolved,

"That William and Mary, King and Queen of England, be declared King and Queen of Scotland, to hold the Crown and royal dignity of the said kingdom, to them the said King and Queen during their lives, and the longer liver of them ; and that the sole and full exercise of the power be only in and exercised by him the said King, in the names of the said King and Queen, during their joint lives ;

and after their deceases, that the said Crown and royal dignity be to the heirs of the body of the said Queen; which failing, to the Princess Anne of Denmark, and the heirs of her body; which also failing, to the heirs of the body of the said William, King of England. And then prayed the said King and Queen to accept the same accordingly." Which being accepted by their Majesties, they were proclaimed King and Queen of Scotland the same day that they were crowned King and Queen of England.

The above-mentioned Acts of Settlement of the respective Crowns of England and Scotland ought to be written in the hearts of every true Briton, and engraven on columns of brass, to be erected in all the cities and boroughs of this island, that posterity may know how much their ancestors suffered, and how much more they were in danger of suffering, from a Popish prince; and that they may with gratitude reverence the memory of their glorious deliverer the immortal King William, to whom, under God, are owing whatever rights, whether religious or civil, they or their latest posterity shall enjoy.

Thus appear the causes each nation had for the late Revolution, and the just reasons for limiting the entail of their respective Crowns in the manner above mentioned.

They at that time doubtless hoped they should

for ever be made happy in a descent of Protestant princes, either from the late Queen Mary, the Princess Anne of Denmark, or the late King William, and therefore saw no necessity for extending the limitation further; but the death of that incomparable Princess, the late Queen Mary, on the 28th of December, 1694, followed by the death of that hopeful Royal infant the Duke of Gloucester, the only surviving issue of the Princess of Denmark, on the 29th of July, 1700, gave fresh alarms to the English nation.

They saw the entail of the Crown reduced to the lives of the late King William and her present Majesty, then Princess of Denmark.

They saw the hopes of a Popish Jacobite party taking new spirit, and beginning to revive.

They saw a long train of Popish princes of the blood next in descent after the demises of the late King William and the Princess of Denmark without issue; they remembered the danger they had so lately been in from one Popish prince, and therefore thought it high time to take all necessary cautions to prevent the same for the future from a numerous train of Roman Catholic princes, all, or most of whom, were very near in blood to a neighbouring monarch, the most powerful prince in Europe, whose interest, as well as inclination, might engage him to support their pretensions with his whole force.

This prudent foresight gave birth to another Act of Parliament in England in the 12th and 13th years of the reign of the late King William, entitled "An Act for the further limitation of the Crown, and better securing the rights and liberties of the subject." By this Act the most illustrious Princess Sophia, Electress and Duchess Dowager of Hanover, is declared the next in succession in the Protestant line to the Crown of England, after the late King William and the Princess Anne of Denmark, and their respective issue; and that from and after the deceases of his said Majesty and the Princess Anne of Denmark, and the heirs of their respective bodies, the Crown should be, remain, and continue to the said Princess Sophia and the heirs of her body, being Protestants.

And thereunto the Lords Spiritual and Temporal, and Commons, in the name of all the people of this realm, did most humbly and faithfully submit themselves, their heirs, and posterities; and did faithfully promise, that after the deceases of his Majesty and her Royal Highness, and the failure of the heirs of their respective bodies, to stand by, maintain, and defend the said Princess Sophia and the heirs of her body, being Protestants, according to the limitation and succession of the Crown in this Act specified and contained, to the utmost of their powers, with their lives and estates, against all persons whatsoever that shall attempt anything to the contrary.

In the 13th and 14th years of the said King two other Acts of Parliament were made, the one entitled "An Act of attainder of the pretended Prince of Wales of high treason;" whereby it was enacted "That he be attainted of high treason, and suffer pains of death, as a traitor; and that if any subject of England shall, within this realm, or without, after the first of March, 1701, hold, entertain, or keep any intelligence or correspondence, in person or by letters, messages, or otherwise, with the said pretended Prince of Wales, or with any person or persons employed by him, knowing such person to be so employed by him, or shall by bill of exchange, or otherwise, remit or pay any sum or sums of money, for the use or service of the said pretended Prince of Wales, knowing such money to be for such use or service, such person so offending, being lawfully convicted, shall be taken, deemed, and adjudged guilty of high treason, and shall suffer and forfeit as in cases of high treason. And where any offence against this Act shall be committed out of this realm, the same may be alleged, laid, inquired of, and tried in any county of this kingdom of England."

And the other, entitled "An Act for the further security of his Majesty's person, and the succession of the Crown in the Protestant line, and for extinguishing the hopes of the pretended Prince of Wales, and all other pretenders, and their open and secret abettors." Wherein, reciting the said former Acts of Settlement of the Crown, and that the French King, in hopes of disturbing the peace and repose of his Majesty and his kingdoms, and creating divisions therein, had caused the pretended Prince of Wales, to be proclaimed King of England, Scotland, and Ireland, by the name of James the Third; and that the said pretended Prince had assumed the said title, in open defiance of the provisions made for the establishment of the title, and succession of the Crown, by the said several Acts of Parliament; to the intent, therefore, that the said Acts might be for ever inviolably preserved, and that all future questions and divisions, by reason of any pretended titles to the Crown, might be prevented, it was enacted that all and every person and persons, as well Peers as Commoners, that shall bear office, civil or military, or receive pay, fee, or wages, or have command or place of trust from his Majesty, or in the service of his Majesty, Prince George, or Princess Anne of Denmark, all ecclesiastical persons, or members of colleges and halls, of the foundation in either university, being eighteen years old, all persons teaching pupils, all schoolmasters, ushers, preachers, and teachers of separate congregations, persons that shall act as serjeants-at-law, counsellors, advocates, attorneys, solicitors, proctors, clerks, or notaries by practising as such in any court, and all Peers and members of the House of Commons, before they can vote in their respective Houses of Parliament, should be obliged to take the oath hereinafter mentioned, commonly called "The Abjuration Oath," which oath was expressed in the following words :—

"I, A. B., do truly and sincerely acknowledge, profess, testify, and declare, in my conscience, before God and the world, that our Sovereign Lord King William is lawful and rightful King of this realm, and of all other his Majesty's dominions and countries thereunto belonging ; and I do solemnly and sincerely declare that I do believe in my conscience, that the person pretended to be Prince of Wales, during the life of the late King James, and since his decease pretending to be and taking upon himself the style and title of King of England, by the name of James the Third, hath not any right or title whatsoever to the Crown of this realm, or any other the dominions thereunto belonging ; and I do renounce, refuse, and abjure any allegiance or obedience to him. And I do swear that I will bear faith and true allegiance to his Majesty King William, and him will defend, to the utmost of my power, against all traitorous conspiracies and attempts whatsoever, which shall be made against his person, crown, or dignity ; and I will do my best endeavour to disclose and make known to his Majesty, and his successors, all treasons and traitorous conspiracies which I shall know to be against him or any of them; and I do faithfully promise, to the utmost of my power, to support, maintain, and defend the limitation and succession of the Crown, against him the said James and all other persons whatsoever, as the same is and stands limited (by an Act entitled 'An Act declaring the rights and liberties of the subject, and settling the succession of the Crown') to his Majesty, during his Majesty's life, and after his Majesty's decease to the Princess Anne of Denmark, and the heirs of her body, being Protestants, and, for default of such issue, to the heirs of the body of his Majesty, being Protestants; and as the same by one other Act, entitled 'An Act for the further limitations of the Crown, and better securing the rights and liberties of the subject,' is and stands limited after the decease of his Majesty and the Princess Anne of Denmark; and, for default of issue of the said Princess and of his Majesty respectively, to the Princess Sophia, Electress and Duchess Dowager of Hanover, and the heirs of her body, being Protestants. And all these things I do plainly and sincerely acknowledge, and swear, according to these express words by me spoken, and according to the plain and common sense and understanding of these same words, without any equivocation, mental evasion, or secret reservation whatsoever; and I do make this recognition, acknowledgment, abjuration, renunciation, and promise, heartily, willingly, and truly, upon the true faith of a Christian. So help me God."

And it was thereby also enacted, that if any person or persons, at any time after the 25th day of March, 1702, should compass or imagine the death of her Royal Highness the Princess Anne of Denmark, or endeavour to deprive or hinder her from succeeding to the Imperial Crown of this realm, and the dominions and territories thereunto belonging, after the demise of his Majesty, and the same maliciously, advisedly, and directly shall attempt, by any overt act or deed, every such offence shall be adjudged high treason, and the offender and offenders therein, their abettors, procurers, and counsellors, and all and every their aiders and comforters, knowing the said offence to be done, being thereof convicted, or attainted, according to the laws and statutes of this realm, shall be deemed and adjudged traitors, and shall suffer pains of death, and all losses and forfeitures, as in cases of high treason.

Thus our great deliverer accomplished his work.

He would have thought it but half done if he had delivered only one generation from Popery and slavery; and therefore made it his whole care, and spent the last remains of his invaluable life, in contriving how the most pure religion and the best laws in the universe might be transmitted to late posterity.

The last mentioned Acts of Parliament, and the legacy that great Prince left the English nation, infinitely more valuable than if he had, without them, left palaces and principalities to each of his subjects.

The memory of that great benefactor to mankind will always be dear to every Briton, who loves the religion and laws of his country, and is an enemy to Popery and arbitrary power, and to every man who knows the happiness of a limited monarchy, circumscribed and fenced about with the bulwarks of laws which equally guard the subject from the invasion of the prince and the prince from the insults of the subject.

His vigilance was not confined to his kingdom of England; the happiness of the kingdom of Scotland was equally his care and study. He zealously attempted to have had the succession to the Crown of that kingdom settled also on the House of Hanover, in the same manner as that of England was settled, and to have united both kingdoms; but these high benefits were reserved by Heaven to be numbered amongst the glories of her present Majesty's reign, a reign attended with so many victories obtained by her arms abroad, under the conduct of her renowned general, the Duke of Marlborough; and with so many acts of benevolence at home, by the advice of the best and wisest council that ever prince employed, that, as it has excelled the transactions of all former ages, so it will be a lasting pattern for the imitation of all which shall succeed.

Her Majesty was but just seated on her throne, when, with the same goodness towards her subjects, in the first year of her reign, she gives the Royal assent to an Act of Parliament, intituled " An Act for enlarging the time for taking the Oath of Abjuration ; and also for recapacitating and indemnifying such persons as have not taken the same by the time limited, and shall take the same by a time to be appointed ; and for the further security of her Majesty's person, and the succession of the Crown in the Protestant line, and for extinguishing the hopes of the pretended Prince of Wales, and all other pretenders, and their open and secret abettors ;" in which, amongst other things, it is enacted : " That if any person or persons, at any time after the first day of March, 1702, shall endeavour to deprive or hinder any person who shall be the next in succession to the Crown, for the time being, according to the limitations in an Act, intituled 'An Act declaring the rights and liberties of the subject, and settling the succession of the Crown ;' and according to another Act, intituled ' An Act for the further limitation of the Crown, and better securing the rights and liberties of the subject,' from succeeding after the decease of her Majesty, to the Imperial Crown of this realm, and the dominions and territories thereunto belonging, according to the limitations in the before mentioned Acts, that is to say, such issue of her Majesty's body as shall from time to time be next in succession to the Crown, if it shall please God Almighty to bless her Majesty with issue; and during the time her Majesty shall have no issue, the Princess Sophia, Electress and Duchess Dowager of Hanover; and after the decease of the said Princess Sophia, the next in succession to the Crown, for the time being, according to the limitation of the said Acts; and the same, maliciously, advisedly, and directly shall attempt by any overt act or deed; every such offence shall be adjudged high treason, and the offender or offenders therein, their abettors, procurers, and comforters, knowing the said offence to be done, being thereof convicted or attainted, according to the laws and statutes of this realm, shall be deemed and adjudged traitors, and shall suffer pains of death, and all losses and forfeitures, as in cases of high treason."

Her Majesty in the fourth year of her reign gave the Royal assent to an Act, entitled "An Act for the naturalization of the most excellent Princess Sophia, Electress and Duchess Dowager of Hanover, and the issue of her body;" by which it is enacted, "That the said Princess Sophia, and the issue of her body, and all persons lineally descending from her, born, or hereafter to be born, be, and shall be, to all intents and purposes whatsoever, deemed, taken, and esteemed natural born subjects of this kingdom, as if the said Princess, and the issue of her body, and all persons lineally descending from her, born, or hereafter to be born, had been born within this realm of England, any law, statute, matter, or thing whatsoever to the contrary notwithstanding, with a proviso that every person who shall be naturalized by virtue of this Act, and shall become a Papist, or profess the Popish religion, shall not enjoy any benefit or advantage of a natural born subject of England, but shall be judged an alien."

And in the fourth and fifth year of her Majesty's reign another Act passed the Royal assent, intituled " An Act for the better securing her Majesty's person and government, and of the succession to the Crown of England in the Protestant line ;" by which, amongst other things, it is enacted, "That if any person or persons, from and after the 25th day of March, 1706, shall maliciously, advisedly, and directly, by writing or printing, declare, maintain, and affirm, that our Sovereign Lady the Queen, that now is, is not the lawful or rightful Queen of these realms; or that the pretended Prince of Wales, who now styles himself King of England by the name of James the Third, hath any right or title to the Crown of these realms; or that any other person or persons hath or have any right or title to the same, otherwise than according to an Act of Parliament, made in the first year of their late Majesties King William and Queen

Mary, intituled 'An Act declaring the rights and liberties of the subject, and settling the succession of the Crown;' and one other Act, made in the 12th year of the reign of his said late Majesty King William the Third, intituled 'An Act for the further limitation of the Crown, and better securing the rights and liberties of the subject:'

"Or that the Kings or Queens of England, with and by the authority of the Parliament of England, are not able to make laws and statutes of sufficient force and validity, to limit and bind the Crown of this realm, and the descent, limitation, inheritance, and government thereof, every such person or persons shall be guilty of high treason, and being thereof convicted and attainted, according to the laws and statutes of this realm, shall be deemed and adjudged traitors, and shall suffer pains of death, and all losses and forfeitures, as in case of high treason.

"And that if any person or persons shall, from and after the said 25th day of March, maliciously and directly, by preaching, teaching, or advised speaking, declare, maintain, and affirm, in manner as aforesaid, every such person or persons, being thereof lawfully convicted, shall incur the danger and penalty of præmunire.

"And that the Parliament shall not be dissolved by the death or demise of her Majesty, her heirs or successors; but such Parliament, if sitting at the time of such demise, may proceed to act for six months, and no longer, unless the same shall be sooner prorogued or dissolved by such person to whom the Crown of this realm of England shall come, according to the Acts for limiting and settling the succession above mentioned. And if the said Parliament shall be so prorogued, then it shall meet and sit on the day unto which it shall be prorogued, and continue for the residue of the said six months, unless sooner prorogued or dissolved as aforesaid. And if there be a Parliament in being, at the time of the death of her Majesty, her heirs or successors, but happens to be separated by adjournment or prorogation, such Parliament shall immediately after such demise meet, and act for six months, and no longer, unless the same shall be prorogued or dissolved, as aforesaid. And in case there is no Parliament in being at the time of such demise, that has met and sat, then the last preceding Parliament shall immediately convene, and sit at Westminster, and be a Parliament to continue as aforesaid ; but subject to be prorogued and dissolved as aforesaid.

"That the Privy Council of her Majesty, her heirs, and successors, shall not be dissolved by such death or demise, but shall continue for six months, unless sooner determined by the next successor ;

"Nor shall any office, place, or employment, civil or military, become void by such demise, but continue also for six months, unless the persons enjoying them shall be sooner removed and discharged by the next successor.

"And if her Majesty shall happen to die without issue, the Privy Council shall with all convenient speed cause the next Protestant successor entitled to the Crown of England by virtue of the Acts above mentioned, to be openly and solemnly proclaimed in England and Ireland, in usual manner; and every member thereof wilfully neglecting or refusing to cause such proclamation to be made shall be guilty of high treason; and every officer, by the Privy Council required to make such proclamations, wilfully neglecting or refusing, shall be guilty of and suffer the penalties of high treason.

"And for continuing the administration of the government in the name of such Protestant successor, until her or his arrival in England, the Lord Archbishop of Canterbury, the Lord Chancellor or Lord Keeper, Lord High Treasurer, Lord President of the Council, Lord Privy Seal, Lord High Admiral, and Lord Chief Justice of the Queen's Bench, at that time being, are thereby appointed Lords Justices of England, until such successor arrive or determine their authority.

"And the person to succeed in case of her Majesty's death without issue is empowered at any time during her Majesty's life, by three instruments under her or his hand and seal, to appoint so many natural born subjects of England, as she or he shall think fit, to be added to the above mentioned Lords Justices, to act with them as Lords Justices of England, who, or the major part, not being fewer than five, shall execute the power of Lords Justices.

"The said three instruments to be transmitted into England, to the resident of the person next to succeed (whose credentials shall be enrolled in Chancery), and to the Archbishop of Canterbury, and Lord Chancellor or Lord Keeper, close sealed up ; and after they are so transmitted, shall be severally put into several covers, and severally sealed by such resident, Archbishop, and Chancellor or Keeper, and severally deposited in the hands of such resident, Archbishop, and Chancellor or Keeper. If the next successor shall think fit to revoke or alter such appointment, and shall by three writings of the same tenor, under her or his hand and seal, require the said instruments so deposited to be delivered up, then the persons with whom deposited, their executors, administrators, and every other person, in whose custody the said instruments shall happen to be, shall deliver up the same accordingly. And if any of the said persons with whom the said instruments shall be so deposited shall die or be removed from their respective offices or employments during her Majesty's life, such person or persons, and in case of any of their deaths their executors and administrators respectively, and every other person in whose custody the same shall happen to be, shall with all convenient speed deliver such of them as shall be in his or their custody to the successor or successors of the person or persons so dying or removed; which said several instruments so sealed up and deposited shall immediately after the demise of her Majesty without issue be brought before the Privy Council, where the same shall be forthwith opened and read, and afterwards enrolled in the High Court of Chancery.

"If the persons with whom the said instruments shall be deposited, or others in whose custody the same shall be, after the deceases of any of the said persons, shall open the same, or wilfully neglect or refuse to produce them as aforesaid, such persons shall incur the penalties of præmunire.

"And if all the said instruments shall not be produced before the said Privy Council, then any one of the said instruments so produced shall be as effectual to give such authority as aforesaid to the persons therein named as if all of them had been produced. And if there be not any nomination by such instruments, then the said seven officers above named, or any five of them, are appointed to be Lords Justices of England. And that the Lords Justices of England shall not dissolve the Parliament, continued and ordered to assemble and sit as aforesaid, without express direction from such succeeding Queen or King, and are restrained and disabled from giving the Royal assent to any Bill for the repealing or altering the Act for the Uniformity of Public Prayers and Administration of Sacraments, made 13 & 14 Charles II., under the penalty of high treason. And that the said Lords Justices, before they act in their said offices, shall take the oaths mentioned in an Act made 1 William and Mary, entitled 'An Act for abrogating the Oaths of Allegiance and Supremacy, and appointing other Oaths,' and also the Abjuration Oath, before the Privy Council; and all members of both Houses of Parliament, and every member of the Privy Council, and all officers and persons in any offices, places, or employment, civil or military, who shall be by this Act continued as aforesaid, shall take the said oaths, and do all other acts required by the laws of this realm, to qualify themselves to continue in such their respective places, offices, and employments, within such time and in such manner, and under such penalties and disabilities as they should or ought to do, had they been then newly elected, appointed, constituted, or put into such offices, places, or employments in the usual and ordinary way. And that the Lords Justices shall be deemed as persons executing offices of trust within this kingdom, and shall do all acts requisite by the laws to qualify themselves to be and continue in their said offices, within such times, and in such manner, and under such penalties and disabilities, as in and by the said Acts are required.

"And it is in the said Act provided, amongst other things, that if any of the aforesaid seven offices, other than the office of Lord High Treasurer of England, shall be in commission at the time of such demise of her Majesty, that then the first Commissioner of such respective commission shall be one of the Lords Justices of England. And if there be no Lord High Treasurer of England, and the office of Treasurer of the Exchequer shall be in commission, then the first in that commission shall be one of the Lords Justices of England."

I have here shown what wonderful concern and care appeared, as well in her Majesty and her Parliament, as in the late King William and his, for settling the succession to the Crown of England in the Protestant line. I come now to the Act of Parliament for uniting the kingdoms of England and Scotland in one kingdom, by the name of Great Britain.

This had been unsuccessfully attempted by several of her Majesty's predecessors, but the glory of it was reserved for her Majesty, that she might appear as great in her councils as her arms.

This Act is entitled, "An Act for an Union of the two kingdoms of England and Scotland," and received the Royal assent in the fifth year of the reign of her Majesty. It recites that Articles of Union were agreed on, the 22nd day of July, in the fifth year of her Majesty's reign, by the Commissioners nominated on behalf of the kingdom of England, under the Great Seal of England, dated the 10th day of April then last past, in pursuance of an Act of Parliament made in England in the third year of her Majesty's reign, and the Commissioners nominated on the behalf of the kingdom of Scotland, under the Great Seal of Scotland, dated the 27th day of February, in the fourth year of her Majesty's reign, in pursuance of the 4th Act of the third session of the then present Parliament of Scotland, to treat of and concerning a union of the said kingdoms; and reciting that an Act had passed in the Parliament of Scotland, the 16th day of January, in the fifth year of her Majesty's reign, wherein it is mentioned that the estates of Parliament, considering the said Articles of Union of the two kingdoms, had agreed to and approved thereof with some additions and explanations, and that her Majesty had passed in the same session of Parliament an Act, entitled "Act for securing of the Protestant Religion and Presbyterian Church Government," which was appointed to be inserted in any Act ratifying the treaty, and expressly declared to be a fundamental and essential condition of the said treaty or union in all times coming;

The tenor of which Articles, as ratified and

approved of, is at large recited in the said Act of Union. It concerns our present purpose to mention only the first and second.

Article I.

That the two kingdoms of England and Scotland shall, upon the first day of May, which shall be in the year 1707, and for ever after, be united into one kingdom, by the name of Great Britain, and that the ensigns armorial of the said United Kingdom be such as her Majesty shall appoint, and the crosses of St. George and St. Andrew be conjoined in such manner as her Majesty shall think fit, and used in all flags, banners, standards, and ensigns, both at sea and land.

Article II.

That the succession to the monarchy of the United Kingdom of Great Britain, and of the dominions thereto belonging, after her most sacred Majesty, and in default of issue of her Majesty, be, remain, and continue to the most excellent Princess Sophia, Electress and Duchess Dowager of Hanover, and the heirs of her body being Protestants, upon whom the Crown of England is settled by an Act of Parliament made in England in the twelfth year of the reign of his late Majesty King William the Third, entitled "An Act for the further limitation of the Crown, and better securing the rights and liberties of the subject;" and that all Papists, and persons marrying Papists, shall be excluded from and for ever incapable to inherit, possess, or enjoy the Imperial Crown of Great Britain, and the dominions thereunto belonging, or any part thereof; and in every such case the Crown and Government shall from time to time descend to and be enjoyed by such person, being a Protestant, as should have inherited and enjoyed the same, in case such Papist, or person marrying a Papist, was naturally dead, according to the provision for the descent of the Crown of England, made by another Act of Parliament in England, in the first year of the reign of their late Majesties King William and Queen Mary, entitled "An Act declaring the rights and liberties of the subject, and settling the succession of the Crown."

But this point is of so great consequence, that I must beg leave to repeat the history and progress of it, which was thus.

Her Majesty was empowered by two several Acts of Parliament, one of the late kingdom of England and the other of the late kingdom of Scotland, to appoint Commissioners for each kingdom, to treat of a union of the two kingdoms; but it was expressly provided in each Act that the Commisioners should not treat of or concerning the alteration of the worship, discipline, or government of the Church in either kingdom.

The Commisioners were accordingly appointed by her Majesty, and twenty-five Articles were agreed upon between them, which Articles were approved and ratified by two several Acts of Parliament of the said late kingdoms of England and Scotland, in which said Acts each kingdom provided for the preservation of the worship, discipline, and government of its respective Church, within their respective parts of the United Kingdom of Great Britain, and each Act of Parliament for the preservation of the said Churches were agreed to be taken as a fundamental condition of the union, and to be repeated and inserted in any Act of Parliament for agreeing to the said treaty or union betwixt the two kingdoms; and it was expressly enacted in each of the said Acts, "that the said Articles and Acts should be and continue in all time coming the sure and perpetual foundation of a complete and entire union of the two kingdoms of England and Scotland."

After which an Act of Parliament of the United Kingdom of Great Britain was passed, entitled "An Act for an Union of the two Kingdoms of England and Scotland;" wherein, reciting the said twenty-five Articles of the Union, ratified and confirmed by the respective Acts of Parliament of the kingdoms of England and Scotland, and inserting the said Acts of Parliament for preserving the worship, discipline, and government of the respective

Churches of each kingdom, it is thereby enacted that the said Acts of Parliament of England and Scotland, for securing their respective Churches, and the said Articles of Union, so as aforesaid ratified, approved, and confirmed, be, and continue in all times coming, the complete and entire union of the two kingdoms of England and Scotland.

The words, "so as aforesaid ratified, approved, and confirmed," are very material, and ought to be carefully observed, because some of the said Articles are made entire and absolute, and others give a power to the Parliament of Great Britain to alter the same; so that these words, "so as aforesaid ratified, approved, and confirmed," must be taken "reddendo singula singulis," that is, such of the said Articles as express no power to the Parliament of Great Britain to alter them shall remain entire, and such as carry a power of alteration by the Parliament of Great Britain are not so sacred.

Amongst the Articles that carry no such express power with them is the second Article for settling the succession of the Crown of Great Britain on the House of Hanover; so that I humbly offer it to every good subject's consideration, whether this Article is not as firm as the Union itself, and as the settlement of Episcopacy in England and Presbytery in Scotland.

These were the sacred terms and stipulations

made between the two late kingdoms of England and Scotland, and upon which both kingdoms, by the legal representatives, consented to be dissolved and exist no longer, "but be resolved into, and united in one kingdom, by the name of Great Britain."

The powers that made this happy union, the Parliaments of England and Scotland, have no longer a being; and therefore that union, in the express terms thereof, must remain inviolable. The union would be infringed should there be any deviation from these Articles, and what consequences that would have no good subject can think of without horror; for, as I humbly presume there is no possibility of returning into the same state as we were in before this union, it is wild and extravagant to suppose it can be peaceably broken. Two warlike nations that should separate, after being under solemn obligations of perpetual union, would, like two private men of spirit that had broken friendship, have ten thousand nameless and inexplicable causes of anger boiling in their bosoms, which would render them incapable of living quiet neighbours, and one of them must be brought very low, or neither of them could live in peace or safety. What I mean is, that common sense and the nature of things would make one expect that nothing less than a war could attend the dissatisfactions of such a rupture. It becomes the Englishmen in generosity to be more particularly careful in preserving this union.

For the late kingdom of Scotland had as numerous a nobility as England, and the representatives of their Commons were also very numerous. They have by the Articles of Union consented to send only sixteen Peers and forty-five Commons to the Parliament of Great Britain, which hath the same number of Lords and Commons for England that were before the union; so that the Scots representatives can make no stand in the defence of all or any of the Articles of the Union, should they be opposed by such unequal numbers of the Lords and Commons of England; and therefore it is most plain, from the impotence in which so many wise and able men of the Scotch nation left themselves in these particulars, that they understood the points of religion in England and Scotland respectively, the succession to the Crown of Great Britain, and all other Articles of the Union were never to be controverted.

To guard and protect this settlement of the Crown of the United Kingdom of Great Britain in the Protestant line, an Act of Parliament of the United Kingdom passed in the sixth year of her Majesty's reign, intituled "An Act for the security of her Majesty's person and government, and of the succession to the Crown of Great Britain in the Protestant line," by which the provisions in the before mentioned Act, entitled "An Act for the better security of her Majesty's person and government, and of the succession to the Crown of England in the Protestant line," are extended throughout the whole United Kingdom. It is in effect a repetition of that Act, with proper alterations for that purpose. "So that now throughout Great Britain this Act hath made it high treason for any person maliciously, advisedly, and directly, by writing or printing, to maintain and affirm that our Sovereign Lady the Queen, that now is, is not the lawful and rightful Queen of these realms; or that the pretended Prince of Wales, who now styles himself King of Great Britain, or King of England, by the name of James the Third, or King of Scotland, by the name of James the Eighth, hath any right or title to the Crown of these realms; or that any other person or persons hath or have any right or title to the same, otherwise than according to an Act of Parliament made in England, in the first year of the reign of their late Majesties King William and Queen Mary, entitled 'An Act declaring the rights and liberties of the subject, and settling the succession of the Crown,' and one other Act made in England, in the twelfth year of the reign of his said late Majesty King William the Third, entitled 'An Act for the further limitation of the Crown, and better securing the rights and liberties of the subject,' and the Acts lately made in England and Scotland, mutually for the union of the two kingdoms; or that the Kings or Queens of this realm, with and by the authority of Parliament, are not able to make laws and statutes of sufficient force and validity to limit and bind the Crown, and the descent, limitation, inheritance, and government thereof, every such person or persons shall be guilty of high treason; and if any person or persons shall maliciously and directly, by preaching, teaching, or advised speaking, declare, maintain, and affirm as aforesaid, such person or persons shall incur the penalty of præmunire."

Thus did our kingdom of Great Britain begin in the fifth year of her Majesty's reign, and in the year of our Lord 1707. And from this great era, to which it is so easy to look back, every Briton may date this happy conclusion: that all the notions of hereditary right, but that of her Majesty and the heirs of her body, and, in default of such issue, that of the most illustrious Princess Sophia, and the heirs of her body, being Protestants, are at an end.

And all this hath been done in so open a manner, and in so expressive and plain terms, that one cannot but think that our Popish or Jacobite party, who have been of late so bold both in writing and speaking against the settlement of the Crown of Great Britain, in the Protestant line, and cannot possibly plead ignorance of these things, must have some unaccountable encouragement for their support. But let me inform every Briton that loves his Queen, religion, laws, and liberties, it is his duty to appear boldly in their defence, and detect and seize those enemies to his country, wherever he finds them. What should any man fear in so just a cause, who acts under the guard and protection of the laws of his country, whilst his opponents act with halters about their necks?

It is not material to mention the grand suspicions of the spurious birth of the pretended Prince of Wales; that it was talked with great assurance by the Papists, that the late King James's Queen was big with a son some months before the pretended birth, for they well knew a daughter would not do their business; that at the time of the pretended birth the Princess Anne, now our most gracious Queen, was at the bath; that the Bishops were clapt up in the tower; that the women about the Queen were Papists; that the presumptive heir was not present; that at the birth of the present French King, the next heir, though a man, was permitted to see the Queen actually delivered; that in our case it might have been done with much more decency had there been a birth, since the next heir was a woman; that the late King James and his Queen owning the Pretender is no argument for his not being spurious, considering the bigotry of that Prince, and the great influence the clergy of the Church of Rome have on their laity; that our own history informs us that the first Queen Mary was prevailed on by her

Popish priests to feign herself with child, to exclude her Protestant sister, the Lady Elizabeth, from the Crown of England; that the imposture had been carried on, and a birth been imposed upon the nation, had not King Philip, her husband, wisely considered that the impostor would not only succeed to the Crown of England, but also to that of Spain, and so prevented it. I say these things are altogether insignificant, they are foreign to the purpose. Be the Pretender who he will, or whoever was his father or mother, it concerns not any Briton: he is an attainted person, an enemy to our Queen and country; and all his aiders and abettors are guilty of high treason.

Now I am upon the subject of this late settlement of the Crown, I cannot forbear to express my wonder that there can be found any Briton weak enough to contend against a power in their own nation which is practised to a much greater degree in other States, and without the least scruple exercised, according to the emergencies of human affairs. How hard is it, that Britain should be debarred the privilege of establishing its own security, even by relinquishing only those branches of the royal line which threaten it with destruction, whilst other nations never scruple, upon less occasions, to go much greater lengths. There have been even in France three different races of their kings; the first began with Pharamond, the second with Charles

Martell, and the third with Hugh Capet; and I doubt whether, if the direct line of the blood royal of France were to be followed, it would make for the title of his present most Christian Majesty. But, to come to fresh instances, in which Great Britain itself hath not been unconcerned, what right, by the contrary rule, could the Duke of Savoy have to the kingdom of Sicily, or the Elector of Bavaria to that of Sardinia? Can Great Britain help to advance men to other thrones, and have no power in limiting its own? Has not Louis the Fourteenth given us fresh instances of such innovations in his own family? Or can men think he is not in earnest in excluding his grandson the King of Spain, and his descendants, from the Crown of France, and the Dauphin and Duke of Berri, and their descendants, from the Crown of Spain? And if such sacred things as kingdoms themselves may be thus disposed of out of the right line, not by any resignation that can in any equitable sense be called voluntary, but apparently for mere reasons of state and ambition, certainly the English and Scotch, for preservation of religion, liberty, and property, the essential benefits of life, might with more justice settle their Crown in the Protestant line in the manner they have done, excluding all the nearer princes of the blood that are Papists.

When I reflect on these many solemn strong barriers of laws and oaths, of policy and religion, of penalties without, and conscience within, methinks all fear vanisheth before them. It seems a phantom only, that disappears with the light; and I begin to hope it is as ridiculous and groundless as the artifice of some men endeavours to represent it. But my thoughts will not let me rest here; I ask myself, before I am aware, what are the marks of a lasting security? What are our tempers and our hearts at home? In what hands is power lodged abroad? Are our unnatural divisions our strength? Or is it nothing to us which of the Princes of Europe hath the longest sword? The powerful hand that deals out crowns and kingdoms all around us, may it not in time reach out a king to us too? Are there no pretensions to our Crown that can ever be revived? Or are Popery and ambition become tame and quiet neighbours?

These uneasy questions are enough to satisfy any Briton that we can neither know our security, nor be sensible of our danger, from any partial view of our condition, or from appearances on one side only. Our condition cannot be judged of but from the circumstances of the affairs of Europe in general, as well as of Great Britain in particular.

That I may represent this with the more advantage, and put everything in its proper view, I cannot but look back on the glorious scene some past years presented us with, a scene too glorious indeed to be forgotten, and yet too affecting to be remembered.

Ambition, tyranny and oppression seemed not long ago to be just taking their leave of this part of the world, and ready to give place to honour, liberty and justice. The French for near an age had been always triumphant in their encroachments on their neighbours; from the number of their troops, their early taking the field, the remissness of their enemies, joined with their happy manner of interpreting the sense of their leagues and treaties, they had always succeeded in everything they undertook; the long series of their good fortune made them arrogate to themselves the titles of intrepid and invincible; but the destined time came, and they were to their costs as fully convinced of their mistake by the bravery of the British troops, under the conduct of her Majesty's late general, the great Duke of Marlborough.

As this wonderful instrument of Providence carried in his fortune the fate of the British people, who can forbear to run over the good events that happened under him, and the honours paid to him; both which are recited not as they are personal to himself, but as they concern the British name and nation, which he represented.

The first thing that meets my imagination is, the French army broken, routed, flying over the plains of Blenheim, and choosing rather to throw themselves headlong into the Danube than face about upon their conqueror. I see the just honours done him by the Emperor and the whole empire; I hear him with loud acclamations acknowledged the deliverer of Europe. He is introduced into the College of Princes, and takes possession of the principality of Mindelheim. Triumphant columns are erected in the plains of Blenheim, recording the seasonable assistance of the British arms and the glories of that immortal day.

The British leader returns from the Danube to the Rhine ; he and his brave companions are the delight of the nations through whom they march, and are styled their good, their guardian angels. After passing so many different nations in a triumphant manner, he lands in his own country, a humble, unattended subject, honouring and adorning his nation by privacy and modesty at home, much more than by the highest triumphs and ostentations abroad.

The Queen and Senate pass in religious pomp to thank the Almighty for victory over the then common oppressor. But the prospect does not end here : the plains of Ramillies are a new scene of glory to the Confederate arms, and a second happy day ends the bondage of many cities !

His most Christian Majesty conceives new hopes from changing his generals, and from the conduct of Vendôme promises himself to repair the diminution of his glory by Villeroy.

The branches of his Royal family, the Dukes of Burgundy and Berri, are to animate the soldiery by their presence; but Vendôme, Burgundy, and Berri are not strong enough for the genius of the Duke of Marlborough at Oudenard.

The French still change their general, and Villars is in command. He soon shares the same fate with his predecessors, by being beaten out of his camp by an inferior number of troops: a camp so strong, by nature and art that, as none but the Duke of Marlborough would have attempted it, so none but that consummate captain at the head of his brave countrymen could have succeeded in it. In short, methinks I see Ostend, Menin, Lisle, Tournay, Mons, Aire, Douay, and innumerable other towns, held impregnable, all besieged, taken, and restored to their lawful Prince and ancient liberties.

The English General, during the course of ten campaigns, besieged no town but what he took, attacked no army but what he routed, and returned each year with the humility of a private man.

If beating the enemy in the field, and being too vigilant for their councils in foreign Courts, were effectual means towards ending the war, and reducing them to a condition too low for giving fresh disturbance to Europe, the Duke of Marlborough took just measures; but, however unaccountable it may appear to posterity, that General was not permitted to enjoy the fruits of his glorious labour; but, as France changed her generals for want of success in their conduct, so Britain changes hers after an uninterrupted series of conquest. The minds of the people, against all common sense, are debauched with impressions of the Duke's affectation of prolonging the war for his own glory; and his adversaries attack a reputation which could not well be impaired without sullying the glory of Great Britain itself. His enemies were not to be softened by that consideration: he is dismissed, and soon after a suspension of arms between Great Britain and France is proclaimed at the head of the armies. The British, in the midst of the enemy's garrisons, withdraw themselves from their confederates. The French, now no longer having the Britons or their great leader to fear, affect no more strong garrisons and fortified camps, but attack and rout the Earl of Albemarle at Denain, and necessitate the brave Prince Eugene to abandon Landrecy, a place of such importance that it gave entrance into the heart of France, of which the French King was so sensible that, before he was recovered from his fright, he acknowledged he in a manner owed his Crown to the suspension of arms between him and Great Britain. The suspension is followed by a treaty of peace at Utrecht. The peace is concluded between Great Britain and France, and between France and the States-General. The Emperor and the Empire continue the war. I shall not presume to enter into an examination of the articles of peace between us and France; but there can be no crime in affirming (if it be a truth) that the House of Bourbon is at this juncture become more formidable, and bids fairer for a universal monarchy and to engross the whole trade of Europe, than it did before the war.

All the world knows with what frankness the Dutch have been treated to deliver up Traerbach to the Imperialists, as an expedient for the French to besiege it, because, forsooth, it lay convenient for their incursions upon the Empire. This extravagant demand must give a melancholy prospect to other nations.

The most important article between France and England is the demolition of Dunkirk, which they have begun contemptuously and arbitrarily their own way: the mole and harbour, which only are dreadful to us, are yet untouched, and just suspicions given that they ever will be.

Landau and Fribourg are taken; and in case there is no intermediate peace, which may still be more immediately fatal to us, two hundred thousand French may be ready in the spring to invade the Empire, and restore the Duke of Bavaria to his forfeited dominions.

These incidents happen when the capital of Austria, the residence of his Imperial Majesty, is visited with the plague. The male line of that house is likely to terminate in himself; and should it please God to take him off, and no King of the Romans chosen, a Prince of the House of Bourbon would probably bid fair for the Imperial dignity, after which day farewell liberty! Europe would be French.

But the scene is not yet closed. Portugal, which during the war supplied to us the place of Spain, by sending us vast quantities of gold in exchange for our woollen manufactures, has only at present a suspension of arms for its protection, which suspension may possibly last no longer than till the Catalonians are reduced; and who knows but the old pretensions of Spain to Portugal may be then revived? I mention the Catalonians, but who can name the Catalonians without a tear! Brave, unhappy people! Drawn into the war by the encouragement of the maritime powers, from which only a nation encompassed by land by France and Spain could hope for relief and protection, now abandoned and exposed to the resentment of an enraged Prince, whose person and interest they have always opposed; and yet still so fond of their ancient liberties, that, though hemmed up in a nook of land by the forces of the two Crowns, and closely besieged in Barcelona, they choose rather, like their countrymen, the famous Saguntines of old, to perish with their wives and children, than live in slavery. Did the French King, with a conquering sword in his hand, ever abandon the least and most inconsiderable of all his allies? No. When these very Catalonians had assisted him against the King of Spain, he did not give up his power of treating till he had made the most honourable conditions for them; not a single man amongst them was then hurt either in his person or privileges. But now, poor unhappy Catalonians, worthy of a better fate! Good and gracious God! To whom shall be attributed the loss of this brave people! Dreadful the doom of those who shall in thy sight be esteemed their destroyers.

But, to bring these several facts and circumstances home, we must observe, that the person who seems to be the most favoured by the French King in the late treaties is the Duke of Savoy, who is made King of Sicily; and, considering also the enlargement of his territories on the Continent by cession from the Emperor, is become the most powerful Prince in Italy. This Prince put in his claim to the Crown of England, in the right of his wife, a daughter of the late Duchess of Orleans, sister to our late King Charles the Second, at the time of settling the Crown of England on the House of Hanover. This Prince, a man of as great address and capacity as any now living, is supposed to have entered into a secret and strict alliance with the House of Bourbon, and may therefore very well add to our fears of a Popish successor.

Things standing thus, and the House of Bourbon

being in the actual possession of France and Spain, bidding fair for the conquest of Germany, or in peace and good understanding with it; what have Great Britain and Holland to hope from but the mercy of France? What else have we to prevent the Pretender being imposed on us, when France shall think fit—nay, in failure of one pretender, he has in his quiver a succession of them; the Duchess of Savoy, or her sons, or the Dauphin her grandson. The last named cannot be many years from the throne of France.

In the next place, how are we disposed at home for the reception of such an attempt? The passions of many, which were raised so high by an impudent suggestion of the Church's danger, seem to have subsided into a lethargic unconcern for everything else; harmless men are ashamed to own how grossly they have been imposed upon, and, instead of resenting the abuse, are willing to overlook it, with a certain reluctance against being moved at anything else, lest they should fall into the mortification of being misled a second time. Many, who are above being blinded by popular noise and outcry, yet seem to think the warmth and zeal of a public spirit to be little better than a romantic heat of brain. Treasonable books lately dispersed amongst us, that have apparently struck at the Protestant succession in the House of Hanover, have passed almost without observation from the generality of the people; subtle queries have been published about the birth of a certain person, which certain person everybody knows to be intended for the Pretender; the author of "The Conduct of the Allies" has dared to drop insinuations about altering the succession; and a late treasonable book, on the subject of Hereditary Right, has published the will of King Henry the Eighth, which seems to be intended as a pattern for the like occasion.

The conversion of the Pretender to our religion has been occasionally reported and contradicted, according to the reception it met with among the soft fools who give that gross story a hearing. The unhappy Prince, whose son the Pretender calls himself, is a memorable instance how much such conversions are to be depended upon. King James, when Duke of York, for a long time professed himself a Protestant; and even not long before his succession to the Crown, several persons had actions brought against them for saying he was a Papist, and exorbitant damages given and recovered. In a word, from the practice of all Papists that have come to Protestant thrones upon pretence of embracing the reformed religion, we have reason to believe they have dispensations from Rome to personate anything for the service of that Church. A Popish Prince will never think himself obliged by the most solemn, even the Coronation Oath, to his Protestant subjects. All oaths are as insignificant, and as soon forgotten, as the services done by such Protestant subjects.

King James, when Duke of York, was preserved from the Bill of Exclusion by the Church of England, and particularly its bishops. When he came to the Crown, the Church was soon insulted and outraged by him, and her prelates committed to the Tower.

Has not a neighbouring Prince cruelly treated and banished his Protestant subjects, who preserved the crown on his head?

Did not the Princess Mary promise the men of Suffolk, who joined with her against the Lady Jane Grey, that she would make no alteration in the religion established by her brother, King Edward the Sixth? And yet as soon as she came to the Crown, by the assistance even of Suffolk men, she filled all England, and in a particular manner that county, with the flames of martyrs. The cruelties of that reign were such that multitudes of men, women and children were burnt for being zealous' professors of the Gospel of the Lord Jesus. In short, nothing less than this can be expected from a Popish Prince; both clergy and laity must share the same fate; all universally must submit to the fiery trial, or renounce their religion. Our bishops and clergy must all lose their spiritual preferments, or submit to all antichristian tyranny. And, should they submit to everything, they must notwithstanding part from their wives and children, which, according to the

Church of Rome, are harlots and spurious. The laity, possessed of lands that formerly belonged to the Roman Catholic clergy, must resign their estates, and perhaps be made accountable for the profits received.

What can be more moving, than to reflect upon the barbarous cruelties of Papists beyond all example; and these not accidental, or the sudden effects of passion or provocation, but the settled result of their religion and their consciences.

Above 100,000 men, women and children were murdered in the massacre of Ireland. How hot and terrible were the late persecutions of the Protestants in France and Savoy! How frequent were the massacres of Protestants through the whole kingdom of France, when they were under the protection of the then laws of that country! How barbarous, in a particular manner, was the massacre of Paris, at the marriage of the King of Navarre, the French King's grandfather, a Protestant, with the sister of Charles the Ninth, where the famous Admiral of France, the great Coligny, the glorious asserter of the Protestant interest, was inhumanly murdered, and the body of that hero dragged naked about the streets, and this by the direction of the King himself, who had but just before most treacherously given him, from his own mouth, assurance of his protection! Ten thousand Protestants, without distinction of quality, age, or sex, were put to the sword at the same time; the King of Navarre himself narrowly escaped this disaster, his mother the Queen of Navarre having not long before been poisoned by the same faction.

These are some instances of what must ever be expected. No obligations on our side, no humanity or natural probity on theirs, are of any weight; their very religion forces them, upon pain of damnation, to forget and cancel the former, and to extinguish all remains of the latter. Good God! To what are they reserved, who have nothing to expect but what such a religion can afford them? It cannot therefore be too often repeated. We should consider, over and over again, that should the chain of the Protestant succession be once broke in upon, though the Pretender should be laid aside, the next of the blood royal is the Duchess of Savoy; after her, her two sons; after them, the present Dauphin of France; the next in succession to him, the Queen of Spain, and her heirs; in default of them, the Duke of Orleans; and his heirs, and most of the other Princes of the blood of France, all Papists, who may be enabled to demand preference to the House of Hanover; so that, besides the probability of this kingdom being united to, and made a province of France, the train of Popish Princes is so great, that, if one should not complete the utter extirpation of our religion, laws, and liberties, the rest would certainly do it.

And here I cannot but add what is still of more importance, and ought to be the most prevalent of all arguments, that should there be the least hopes given to a Popish successor, the life of her Majesty will certainly be in most imminent danger; for there will never be wanting bloody zealots of that persuasion that will think it meritorious to take away her Majesty's life to hasten the accession of such a successor to her throne.

The only preservation against these terrors are the laws before-mentioned relating to the settlement of the Imperial Crown of Great Britain Thanks be to Heaven for that settlement. The Princess Sophia, and the heirs of her body, being Protestants, are the successors to her present Majesty, upon her demise without issue. The way is plain before our eyes, guarded on the right hand and on the left by all the sanctions of God and man, and by all the ties of law and conscience. Let those who act under the present settlement, and yet pretend to dispute for an absolute hereditary right, quiet themselves with the arguments they have borrowed from Popery, and teach their own consciences the art of dispensing with the most solemn oath to this Establishment, whilst they think themselves bound only till opportunity shall serve to introduce another. God be thanked! neither we, nor our cause, stand in need of such detestable prevarication. Our cause is our happiness. Our oaths are our judgment and inclination. Honour and affection call us, without the solemnity of an oath, to defend such an Establishment; but with it we have every motive that can influence the mind of man. The terrors of God, added to the demands of our country, oblige and constrain us to let our hearts and our hands follow our wishes and our consciences; and, out of regard to our Queen, our religion, our country, our liberty, and our property, to maintain and assert the Protestant succession in the illustrious House of Hanover: it is no time to talk with hints and innuendoes, but openly and honestly to profess our sentiments, before our enemies have completed and put their designs in execution against us. As divided a people as we are, those who are for the House of Hanover are infinitely superior, in number, wealth, courage, and all arts, military and civil, to those that are in the contrary interest; besides which, we have the laws—I say the laws—on our side. And those who by their practices, whatever their professions are, have discovered themselves enemies to the constitution and friends to the Pretender, cannot make a step farther without being guilty of treason, without standing in broad daylight confessed criminals against their injured Queen and country.

When the people were in a ferment, when faction ran high, with irresistible prepossessions against everything in its former channel, sanguine men might conceive hopes of leading them their own way. But the building erected upon that quicksand, the favour of the multitude, will sink, and be swallowed up by that treacherous ground on which the foundation was laid.

It is easy to project the subversion of a people when men see them unaccountably turned for their own destruction; but not so easy to effect that ruin when they are come to themselves, and are sensibly and reasonably affected with thoughts for their preservation. We cannot help it, if so many thousands of our brave brethren, who laid down their lives against the power of France, have died in vain; but we may value our own lives dearly, like honest men. Whatever may befall the glory and wealth of Great Britain, let us struggle to the last drop of our blood for its religion and liberty. The banners under which we are to enter this conflict, whenever we are called to it, are the laws mentioned in this discourse; when we do not keep them in sight, we have no colours to fly to, no discipline to preserve us, but are devoted, and have given ourselves up to, slaughter and confusion.

While we act manfully under them, we have reason to expect the blessing and assistance of Heaven on its own cause, which it has so manifestly acknowledged to be such, by our many wonderful deliverances, when all human assistances and ordinary means of succour seemed irrevocably removed. We have no pretensions to the Divine favour, but from our firm adherence to that settlement, which He has, by so many wonders and blessings, after such great difficulties and misfortunes, bestowed upon us, and which we have in his sight, and with the invocation of his sacred Name, after preparing ourselves at his altar, so frequently and solemnly sworn to defend. This plain, unperplexed, unalterable rule for our conduct is visibly the work of his hand to a favoured people. Her Majesty's Parliamentary title, and the Succession in the illustrious House of Hanover, is the Ark of God to Great Britain, and, like that of old, carries death to the profane hand that shall dare to touch it.

HISTORIC DOUBTS

RELATIVE TO

NAPOLEON BUONAPARTE.

"Is not the same reason available in theology and in politics? . . . Will you follow truth but to a certain point?"

Vindication of Natural Society, by a late noble writer.

Historic Doubts Relative to Napoleon Buonaparte.

Long as the public attention has been occupied by the extraordinary personage from whose ambition we are supposed to have so narrowly escaped, the subject seems to have lost scarcely anything of its interest. We are still occupied in recounting the exploits, discussing the character, inquiring into the present situation, and even conjecturing as to the future prospects of Napoleon Buonaparte.

Nor is this at all to be wondered at, if we consider the very extraordinary nature of those exploits and of that character, their greatness and extensive importance, as well as the unexampled strangeness of the events, and also that strong additional stimulant, the mysterious uncertainty that hangs over the character of the man. If it be doubtful whether any history (exclusive of such as is avowedly fabulous) ever attributed to its hero such a series of wonderful achievements compressed into so small a space of time, it is certain that to no one were ever assigned so many dissimilar characters. It is true indeed that party prejudices have drawn a favourable and an unfavourable portrait of almost every eminent man; but, amidst all the diversities of colouring, something of the same general outline is always distinguishable, and even the virtues in the one description bear some resemblance to the vices of another; rashness, for instance, will be called courage, or courage rashness; heroic firmness and obstinate pride will correspond in the two opposite descriptions, and in some leading features both will agree. Neither the friends nor the enemies of Philip of Macedon or of Julius Cæsar ever questioned their *courage* or their *military skill*. With Buonaparte, however, it has been otherwise. This obscure Corsican adventurer—a man, according to some, of extraordinary talents and courage; according to others, of very moderate abilities and a rank coward—advanced rapidly in the French army, obtained a high command, gained a series of important victories, and, elated by success, embarked in an expedition against Egypt, which was planned and conducted, according to some, with the most consummate skill, according to others, with the utmost wildness and folly. He was unsuccessful, however; and, leaving the Army of Egypt in a very distressed situation, he returned to France, and found the nation, or at least the army, so favourably disposed towards him, that he was enabled, with the utmost ease, to overthrow the existing Government, and obtain for himself the supreme power; at first under the modest appellation of Consul, but afterwards with the more sounding title of Emperor. While in possession of this power, he overthrew the most powerful coalitions of the other European States against him, and, though driven from the sea by the British fleets, overran nearly the whole Continent, triumphant. Finishing a war, not unfrequently, in a single campaign, he entered the capitals of most of the hostile potentates, deposed and created kings at his pleasure, and appeared the virtual sovereign of the chief part of the Continent, from the frontiers of Spain to those of Russia. Even those countries we find him invading with prodigious armies, defeating their forces, penetrating to their capitals, and threatening their total subjugation; but at Moscow his progress is stopped: a winter of unusual severity, co-operating with the efforts of the Russians, totally destroys his enormous host; and the German sovereigns throw off the yoke, and combine to oppose him. He raises another vast army, which is also ruined at Leipsic; and again another, with which, like a second Antæus, he for some time maintains himself in France, but is finally defeated, deposed, and banished to the island of Elba, of which the sovereignty is conferred on him. Thence he returns, in about nine months, at the head of six hundred men, to attempt the deposition of King Louis, who had been peaceably recalled. The French nation declare in his favour, and he is reinstated without a struggle. He raises another great army to oppose the Allied Powers, which is totally defeated at Waterloo; he is a second time deposed, surrenders to the British, and is placed in confinement at the island of St. Helena. Such is the outline of the eventful history presented to us; in the detail of which, however, there is almost every conceivable variety of statement, while the motives and conduct of the chief actor are involved in still greater doubt, and the subject of still more eager controversy.

In the midst of these controversies, the preliminary question, concerning the *existence* of this extraordinary personage, seems never to have occurred to any one as a matter of doubt; and to show even the smallest hesitation in admitting it would probably be regarded as an excess of scepticism, on the ground that this point has always been taken for granted by the disputants on all sides, being indeed implied by the very nature of their disputes. But is it in fact found that *undisputed* points are always such as have been the most carefully examined as to the evidence on which they rest? that facts or principles which are taken for granted without controversy, as the common basis of opposite opinions, are always themselves established on sufficient grounds? On the contrary, is not any such fundamental point, from the very circumstance of its being taken for granted at once, and the attention drawn off to some other question, likely to be admitted on insufficient evidence, and the flaws in that evidence overlooked? Experience will teach us that such instances often occur: witness the well-known anecdote of the Royal Society, to whom King Charles II. proposed as a question, whence it is that a vessel of water receives no addition of weight from a live fish being put into it, though it does if the fish be dead. Various solutions of great ingenuity were proposed, discussed, objected to, and defended; nor was it till they had been long bewildered in the inquiry that it occurred to them to *try the experiment;* by which they at once ascertained, that the phenomenon which they were striving to account for—which was the acknowledged basis and substratum, as it were, of their debates—had no existence but in the invention of the witty monarch.

Another instance of the same kind is so very remarkable that I cannot forbear mentioning it. It was objected to the system of Copernicus when first brought forward, that if the earth turned on its axis, as he represented, a stone dropped from the summit of a tower would not fall at the foot of it, but at a great distance to the west; *in the same manner as a stone dropped from the masthead of a ship in full sail, does not fall at the foot of the mast,* *but towards the stern.* To this it was answered that a stone being a *part* of the earth, obeys the same laws, and moves with it, whereas it is no part of the ship, of which consequently its motion is independent. This solution was admitted by some, but opposed by others, and the controversy went on with spirit; nor was it till one hundred years after the death of Copernicus that, the experiment being tried, it was ascertained that the stone thus dropped from the head of the mast, *does* fall at the foot of it! *

Let it be observed that I am not now impugning any one particular point, but merely showing generally that what is *unquestioned* is not necessarily unquestionable; since men will often, at the very moment when they are accurately sifting the evidence of some disputed point, admit hastily, and on the most insufficient grounds, what they have been accustomed to see taken for granted.

The celebrated Hume† has pointed out also the readiness with which men believe, on very slight evidence, any story that pleases their imagination

---

* Οὕτως ἀταλαίπωρος τοῖς πολλοῖς ἡ ζήτησις τῆς ἀληθείας, καὶ ἐπὶ τὰ ἕτοιμα μᾶλλον τρέπονται.—Thucyd. B. i. c. 20.

† "With what greediness are the miraculous accounts of travellers received, their descriptions of sea and land monsters, their relations of wonderful adventures, strange men, and uncouth manners."—Hume's "Essay on Miracles," p. 179, 12mo; p. 185, 8vo, 1767; p. 117, 8vo, 1817.

N.B. In order to give every possible facility of reference, three editions of Hume's Essays have been generally employed: a 12mo, London, 1756, and two 8vo editions.

by its admirable and marvellous character. Such hasty credulity however, as he well remarks, is utterly unworthy of a philosophical mind, which should rather suspend its judgment the more in proportion to the strangeness of the account, and yield to none but the most decisive and unimpeachable proofs.

Let it then be allowed us, as is surely reasonable, just to inquire, with respect to the extraordinary story I have been speaking of, on what evidence we believe it. We shall be told that it is *notorious*—*i.e.*, in plain English, it is very *much talked about;* but as the generality of those who talk about Buonaparte do not even pretend to speak from *their own authority*, but merely to repeat what they have casually heard, we cannot reckon them as in any degree witnesses, but must allow ninety-nine hundredths of what we are told to be mere hearsay, which would not be at all the more worthy of credit even if it were repeated by ten times as many more. As for those who profess to have *personally known* Napoleon Buonaparte, and to have *themselves witnessed* his transactions, I write not for them: *if any such there be,* who are inwardly conscious of the truth of all they relate, I have nothing to say to them, but to beg that they will be tolerant and charitable towards their neighbours who had not the same means of ascertaining the truth, and who may well be excused for remaining doubtful about such extraordinary events, till most unanswerable proofs shall be adduced.

Let us, however, endeavour to trace up some of this hearsay evidence as far towards its source as we are able. Most persons would refer to the *newspapers* as the authority from which their knowledge on the subject was derived; so that, generally speaking, we may say, it is on the testimony of the newspapers that men believe in the existence and exploits of Napoleon Buonaparte.

It is rather a remarkable circumstance, that it is common to hear Englishmen speak of the impudent fabrications of foreign newspapers, and express wonder that any one can be found to credit them, while they conceive that in this favoured land the liberty of the press is a sufficient security for veracity. It is true they often speak contemptuously of such "newspaper stories" as last but a short time; indeed, they continually see them contradicted within a day or two in the same paper, or their falsity detected by some journal of an opposite party; but still, whatever is *long adhered to* and often *repeated*, especially if it also appear in *several different* papers (and this, though they notoriously copy from one another), is almost sure to be generally believed. Whence this high respect which is practically paid to newspaper authority? Do men think that, because a witness has been perpetually detected in falsehood, he may therefore be the more safely believed whenever he is *not* detected? Or does adherence to a story, and frequent repetition of it, render it the more credible? On the contrary, is it not a common remark in other cases, that a liar will generally stand to and reiterate what he has once said, merely because he *has* said it?

Let us, if possible, divest ourselves of this superstitious veneration for everything that appears "in print," and examine a little more systematically the evidence which is adduced.

I suppose it will not be denied that the three following are among the most important points to be ascertained, in deciding on the credibility of witnesses: first, whether they have the means of gaining correct information; secondly, whether they have any interest in concealing truth, or propagating falsehood; and, thirdly, whether they agree in their testimony. Let us examine the present witnesses upon all these points.

First, what means have the editors of newspapers for gaining correct information? We know not, except from their own statements. Besides what is copied from other journals, foreign or British (which is usually more than three-fourths of the news published),* they profess to refer to the authority of

---

* "Suppose a fact to be transmitted through twenty persons, the first communicating it to the second, the second to the third, &c., and let the probability of each testimony be expressed by nine-tenths (that is, suppose that of ten reports made by each witness nine only are true), then, at every time the story passes from one witness to another, the

certain private correspondents abroad. *Who* these correspondents are, what means *they* have of obtaining information, or whether they exist at all, we have no way of ascertaining. We find ourselves in the condition of the Hindoos, who are told by their priests that the earth stands on an elephant, and the elephant on a tortoise, but are left to find out for themselves what the tortoise stands on, or whether it stands on anything at all.

So much for our clear knowledge of the means of *information* possessed by these witnesses; next for the grounds on which we are to calculate on their *veracity*.

Have they not a manifest interest in circulating the wonderful accounts of Napoleon Buonaparte and his achievements, whether true or false? Few would read newspapers if they did not sometimes find wonderful or important news in them; and we may safely say that no subject was ever found so inexhaustibly interesting as the present.

evidence is reduced to nine-tenths of what it was before. Thus, after it has passed through the whole twenty, the evidence will be found to be less than one-eighth."—La Place, " Essay Philosophique sur les Probabilités."

That is, the chances for the fact thus attested being true will be, according to this distinguished calculator, less than one in eight: very few of the common newspaper stories, however, relating to foreign countries, could be traced, if the matter were carefully investigated, up to an actual eye-witness, even through twenty intermediate witnesses; and many of the steps of our ladder would, I fear, prove but rotten. Few of the reporters would deserve to have *one in ten* fixed as the proportion of their false accounts.

It may be urged, however, that there are several adverse political parties of which the various public prints are respectively the organs, and who would not fail to expose each other's fabrications.* Doubtless they would, if they could do so without at the same time exposing *their own;* but identity of interests may induce a community of operations up to a certain point; and, let it be observed, that the object of contention between these rival parties is *who* shall have the administration of public affairs, the control of public expenditure, and the disposal of places; the question, I say, is, not whether the people shall be governed or not, but *by which party* they shall be governed—not whether the taxes shall be paid or not, but *who* shall *receive* them. Now it must be admitted that Buonaparte is a political bugbear most convenient to any administration. "If you do not adopt our measures and reject those of our opponents, Buonaparte will be sure to prevail over you; if you do not submit to the Government, at least under *our* administration, this formidable enemy will take advantage of your insubordination to conquer and enslave you; pay

---

* " I need not mention the difficulty of detecting a falsehood in any private or even public history, at the time and place where it is said to happen; much more where the scene is removed to ever so small a distance. . . . . But the matter never comes to any issue, if trusted to the common method of altercation and debate and flying rumours."—Hume's "Essay on Miracles," p. 195, 12mo; pp. 200, 201, 8vo, 1767; p. 127, 8vo, 1817.

your taxes cheerfully, or the tremendous Buonaparte will take all from you." Buonaparte, in short, was the burden of every song; his redoubted name was the charm which always succeeded in unloosing the purse-strings of the nation. And let us not be too sure, safe as we now think ourselves, that some occasion may not occur for again producing on the stage so useful a personage: it is not merely to naughty children in the nursery that the threat of being "given to Buonaparte" has proved effectual. It is surely probable therefore, that, with an object substantially the same, all parties may have availed themselves of one common instrument. It is not necessary to suppose that for this purpose they secretly entered into a formal agreement—though, by the way, there are reports afloat that the editors of the *Courier* and *Morning Chronicle* hold amicable consultations as to the conduct of their public warfare. I will not take upon me to say that this is incredible; but at any rate it is not necessary for the establishment of the probability I contend for. Neither again would I imply that *all* newspaper editors are utterers of forged stories, "knowing them to be forged;" most likely the great majority of them publish what they find in other papers with the same simplicity that their readers peruse it, and therefore, it must be observed, are not at all more proper than their readers to be cited as authorities.

Still it will be said, that unless we suppose a regularly preconcerted plan, we must at least expect to find great discrepancies in the accounts published; though they might adopt the general outline of facts one from another, they would have to fill up the detail for themselves, and in this, therefore, we should meet with infinite and irreconcilable variety.

Now this is precisely the point I am tending to, for the fact exactly accords with the above supposition, the discordance and mutual contradictions of these witnesses being such as would alone throw a considerable shade of doubt over their testimony. It is not in minute circumstances alone that the discrepancy appears, such as might be expected to appear in a narrative substantially true, but in very great and leading transactions, and such as are very intimately connected with the supposed hero. For instance, it is by no means agreed whether Buonaparte led in person the celebrated charge over the bridge of Lodi (for *celebrated* it certainly is, as well as the siege of Troy, whether either event ever really took place or no), or was safe in the rear, while Augereau performed the exploit: the same doubt hangs over the charge of the French cavalry at Waterloo. It is no less uncertain whether or no this strange personage poisoned in Egypt a hospitalful of his own soldiers, and butchered in cold blood a garrison that had surrendered. But, not to multiply instances, the battle of Borodino, which is represented as one of the greatest ever fought, is unequivocally claimed as a victory by both parties; nor is the question decided at this day. We have official accounts on both sides, circumstantially detailed, in the names of supposed respectable persons professing to have been present on the spot, yet totally irreconcilable. *Both* these accounts *may* be false; but since *one* of them *must* be false, that one (it is no matter which we suppose) proves incontrovertibly this important maxim: that *it is possible for a narrative—however circumstantial—however steadily maintained—however public and however important the events it relates—however grave the authority on which it is published—to be nevertheless an entire fabrication!*

Many of the events which have been recorded were probably believed much the more readily and firmly, from the apparent caution and hesitation with which they were at first published—the vehement contradiction in our papers of many pretended French accounts, and the abuse lavished upon them for falsehood, exaggeration, and gasconade. But is it not possible—is it not indeed perfectly natural—that the publishers of known falsehood should assume this cautious demeanour, and this abhorrence of exaggeration, in order the more easily to gain credit? Is it not also very possible, that those who actually believed what they published may have suspected mere *exaggeration* in stories which were entire *fictions?* Many men have that sort of simplicity, that they think themselves quite secure against being deceived, provided they believe only *part* of the story they hear, when perhaps the whole is equally false. So that perhaps these simple-hearted editors, who were so vehement against lying bulletins and so wary in announcing their great news, were in the condition of a clown who thinks he has bought a great bargain of a Jew, because he has beat down the price, perhaps from a guinea to a crown, for some article that is not really worth a groat.

With respect to the character of Buonaparte, the dissonance is, if possible, still greater. According to some, he was a wise, humane, magnanimous hero—others paint him as a monster of cruelty, meanness, and perfidy; some, even of those who are the most inveterate against him, speak very highly of his political and military ability—others place him on the very verge of insanity. But, allowing that all this may be the colouring of party prejudice (which surely is allowing a great deal), there is one point to which such a solution will hardly apply. If there be anything that can be clearly ascertained in history, one would think it must be the *personal courage* of a *military man;* yet here we are as much at a loss as ever: at the very same times, and on the same occasions, he is described by different writers as a man of undaunted intrepidity, and as an absolute poltroon.

What, then, are we to believe? If we are disposed to credit all that is told us, we must believe in the existence not only of one, but of two or three Buonapartes; if we admit nothing but what is well authenticated, we shall be compelled to doubt of the existence of any.*

It appears, then, that those on whose testimony the existence and actions of Buonaparte are generally believed, fail in all the most essential points on which the credibility of witnesses depends: first, we have no assurance that they have access to correct information; secondly, they have an apparent interest in propagating falsehood; and, thirdly, they palpably contradict each other in the most important points.

Another circumstance which throws additional suspicion on these tales is that the Whig party, as they are called—the warm advocates for liberty, and opposers of the encroachments of monarchical power—have for some time past strenuously espoused the cause and vindicated the character of Buonaparte, who is represented by all as having been, if not a tyrant, at least an absolute despot. One of the most

---

* "We entertain a suspicion concerning any matter of fact when the witnesses *contradict* each other, when they are of a *suspicious* character, when they have an *interest* in what they affirm."—Hume's "Essay on Miracles," p. 172, 12mo; p. 176, 8vo, 1767; p. 113, 8vo, 1817.

forward in this cause is a gentleman who once stood foremost in holding up this very man to public execration—who first published, and long maintained against popular incredulity, the accounts of his atrocities in Egypt. Now that such a course should be adopted, for party purposes, by those who are aware that the whole story is a fiction, and the hero of it imaginary, seems not very incredible; but if they believed in the real existence of this despot, I cannot conceive how they could so forsake their principles as to advocate his cause and eulogise his character.

After all, it may be expected that many who perceive the force of these objections, will yet be loth to think it possible that they and the public at large can have been so long and so greatly imposed upon; and thus it is that the magnitude and boldness of a fraud become its best support: the millions who for so many ages have believed in Mahomet or Brahma, lean, as it were, on each other for support, and not having vigour of mind enough boldly to throw off vulgar prejudices and dare be wiser than the multitude, persuade themselves that what so many have acknowledged must be true. But I call on those who boast their philosophical freedom of thought, and would fain tread in the steps of Hume and other inquirers of the like exalted and speculative genius, to follow up fairly and fully their own principles, and, throwing off the shackles of authority, to examine carefully the evidence of whatever is proposed to them, before they admit its truth. That even in this enlightened age, as it is called, a whole nation may be egregiously imposed upon, even in matters which intimately concern them, may be proved (if it has not been already proved) by the following instance. It was stated in the newspapers, that a month after the battle of Trafalgar an English officer, who had been a prisoner of war, and was exchanged, returned to this country from France, and, beginning to condole with his countrymen on the terrible *defeat* they had sustained, was infinitely astonished to learn that the battle of Trafalgar was a splendid victory : he had been assured, he said, that in that battle the English had been totally defeated, and the French were fully and universally persuaded that such was the fact. Now, if this report of the belief of the French nation was *not* true, the British public were completely imposed upon ; if it *were* true, then both nations were at the same time rejoicing in the event of the same battle as a signal victory to themselves, and consequently one or other at least of these nations must have been the dupes of their Government ; for, if the battle was never fought at all, or was not decisive on either side, in that case *both* parties were deceived. This instance, I conceive, is absolutely demonstrative of the point in question.

"But what shall we say to the testimony of those

many respectable persons who went to Plymouth on purpose, and saw Buonaparte with their own eyes? Must they not trust their senses?" I would not disparage either the eyesight or the veracity of these gentlemen. I am ready to allow that they went to Plymouth for the purpose of seeing Buonaparte—nay, more, that they actually rowed out into the harbour in a boat, and came alongside of a man-of-war, on whose deck they saw a man in a cocked hat, who, *they were told,* was Buonaparte. This is the utmost point to which their testimony goes. How they ascertained that this man in the cocked hat had gone through all the marvellous and romantic adventures with which we have so long been amused, we are not told : did they perceive in his physiognomy his true name and authentic history? Truly this evidence is such as country people give one for a story of apparitions ; if you discover any signs of incredulity, they triumphantly show the very house which the ghost haunted, the identical dark corner where it used to vanish, and perhaps even the tombstone of the person whose death it foretold. Jack Cade's nobility was supported by the same irresistible kind of evidence. Having asserted that the eldest son of Edmund Mortimer, Earl of March, was stolen by a beggar-woman, "became a bricklayer when he came to age," and was the father of the supposed Jack Cade, one of his companions confirms the story, by saying, "Sir, he made a chimney in my father's house, and the bricks are alive at this day to testify it; therefore, deny it not."

Much of the same kind is the testimony of our brave countrymen, who are ready to produce the scars they received in fighting against this terrible Buonaparte. That they fought and were wounded, they may safely testify; and probably they no less firmly *believe* what they were *told* respecting the cause in which they fought; it would have been a high breach of discipline to doubt it, and they, I conceive, are men better skilled in handling a musket than in sifting evidence and detecting imposture; but I defy any one of them to come forward and declare, *on his own knowledge*, what was the cause in which he fought, under whose commands the opposed generals acted, and whether the person who issued those commands did really perform the mighty achievements we are told of.

Let those, then, who pretend to philosophical freedom of inquiry—who scorn to rest their opinions on popular belief, and to shelter themselves under the example of the unthinking multitude, consider carefully, each one for himself, what is the evidence proposed to himself in particular, for the existence of such a person as Napoleon Buonaparte—(I do not mean whether there ever was a person bearing that *name*, for that is a question of no consequence, but whether any such person ever performed all the wonderful things attributed to him). Let him then weigh well the objections to that evidence (of which I have given but a hasty and imperfect sketch), and if he then finds it amount to anything *more* than a probability, I have only to congratulate him on his easy faith.

But the same testimony which would have great weight in establishing a thing intrinsically probable will lose part of this weight in proportion as the matter attested is improbable ; and, if adduced in support of anything that is at variance with uniform experience,* will be rejected at once by all sound reasoners. Let us then consider what sort of a story it is that is proposed to our acceptance. How grossly contradictory are the reports of the different authorities, I have already remarked ; but consider, by itself, the story told by any one of them ; it carries an air of fiction and romance on the very face of it: all the events are great, and splendid, and marvellous†—great armies, great victories, great

---

* "That testimony itself derives all its force from experience seems very certain. . . . The first author we believe, who stated fairly the connection between the evidence of testimony and the evidence of experience, was Hume, in his 'Essay on Miracles,' a work . . . . abounding in maxims of great use in the conduct of life."—*Edinburgh Review*, Sept. 1814, p. 328.

† "Suppose, for instance, that the fact which the testimony endeavours to establish partakes of the extraordinary and the marvellous ; in that case the evidence resulting from the testimony receives a diminution, greater or less, in proportion as the fact is more or less unusual."—Hume's "Essay on Miracles," p. 173, 12mo; p. 176, 8vo, 1767; p. 113, 8vo, 1817.

frosts, great reverses, "hairbreadth 'scapes," empires subverted in a few days—everything happening in defiance of political calculations, and in opposition to the *experience* of past times; everything upon that grand scale so common in epic poetry, so rare in real life, and thus calculated to strike the imagination of the vulgar, and to remind the sober-thinking few of the "Arabian Nights." Every event, too, has that *roundness* and completeness which is so characteristic of fiction; nothing is done by halves; we have *complete* victories—*total* overthrows—*entire* subversion of empires—*perfect* re-establishments of them—crowded upon us in rapid succession. To enumerate the improbabilities of each of the several parts of this history would fill volumes; but they are so fresh in every one's memory, that there is no need of such a detail. Let any judicious man, not ignorant of history and of human nature, revolve them in his mind, and consider how far they are conformable to experience,* our best and only sure guide. In vain will he seek in history for something similar to this wonderful Buonaparte: "nought but himself can be his parallel."

Will the conquests of Alexander be compared with his? *They* were effected over a rabble of

---

* "The ultimate standard by which we determine all disputes that may arise is always derived from experience and observation."—Hume's "Essay on Miracles," p. 172, 12mo; p. 175, 8vo, 1767; p. 112, 8vo, 1817.

effeminate undisciplined barbarians, else his progress would hardly have been so rapid: witness has father Philip, who was much longer occupied in subduing the comparatively insignificant territory of the warlike and civilized Greeks, notwithstanding their being divided into numerous petty States, whose mutual jealousy enabled him to contend with them separately. But the Greeks had never made such progress in arts and arms as the great and powerful States of Europe which Buonaparte is represented as so speedily overpowering. His empire has been compared to the Roman. Mark the contrast: he gains in a few years that dominion, or at least control, over Germany, wealthy, civilized, and powerful, which the Romans in the plenitude of their power could not obtain, during a struggle of as many centuries, against the ignorant half-savages who then possessed it!

Another peculiar circumstance in the history of this extraordinary personage is that, when it is found convenient to represent him as defeated, though he is by no means defeated by halves, but involved in much more sudden and total ruin than the personages of real history usually meet with; yet, if it is thought fit he should be restored, it is done as quickly and completely as if Merlin's rod had been employed. He enters Russia with a prodigious army, which is totally ruined by an unprecedented hard winter—everything relating to this man is *prodigious* and *unprecedented;* yet in a few months we find him entrusted with another great army in Germany, which is also totally ruined at Leipsic, making, inclusive of the Egyptian, the third great army thus totally lost: yet the French are so good-natured as to furnish him with another, sufficient to make a formidable stand in France. He is, however, *conquered, and presented with the sovereignty of Elba.* Surely, by-the-by, some more *probable* way might have been found of disposing of him, till again wanted, than to place him thus on the very verge of his ancient dominions. Thence he returns to France, where he is received with open arms, and enabled to lose a fourth great army at Waterloo. Yet so eager were these people to be a fifth time led to destruction, that it was found necessary to confine *him* in an island some thousand miles off, and to quarter foreign troops upon *them,* lest they should make an insurrection in his favour!* Does any one believe all this, and yet refuse to believe a miracle? Or rather, what is this but a miracle? Is it not a violation of the laws of nature? For surely there are moral laws of nature as well as physical, which, though more liable to exceptions in this or that particular case, are no less

* Ἡ θαύματο πολλά.
Καὶ πού τι καὶ βροτῶν φρένας
ΥΠΕΓ ΤΟΝ ΑΗΛΟΗ ΛΟΓΟΝ
Δεδαιδαλμένοι ψεύδεσι ποικίλοις
Ἐξαπατῶντι μῦθοι.—Pind. "Olymp." I.

true as general rules than the laws of matter, and therefore cannot be violated and contradicted *beyond a certain point*, without a miracle.* Nay, there is

---

* This doctrine, though hardly needing confirmation from authority, is supported by that of Hume: his Eighth Essay is throughout an argument for the doctrine of philosophical "necessity," drawn entirely from the general uniformity observable in the course of nature with respect to the principles of *human conduct*, as well as those of the material universe; from which uniformity, he observes, it is that we are enabled, *in both cases*, to form our judgments by means of *Experience.* "And if," says he, "we would explode any forgery in history, we cannot make use of a more convincing argument, than to prove that the actions ascribed to any person are directly contrary to the course of nature. . . . The veracity of Quintus Curtius is as suspicious when he describes the supernatural courage of Alexander, by which he was hurried on singly to attack multitudes, as when he describes his supernatural force and activity, by which he was able to resist them. So readily and universally do we acknowledge a *uniformity in human motives and actions as well as in the operations of body.*"—Eighth Essay, p. 131, 12mo; p. 85, 8vo, 1817.

Accordingly, in the Tenth Essay, his use of the term "miracle," after having called it "a transgression of a law of nature," plainly shows that he meant to include *human* nature. "No testimony," says he, "is sufficient to establish a miracle, unless the testimony be of such a nature that its falsehood would be more miraculous than the fact which it endeavours to establish." The term "prodigy" also (which he all along employs as synonymous with "miracle") is applied to testimony, in the same manner, immediately after: "In the foregoing reasoning we have supposed . . . . that the falsehood of that testimony would be a kind of prodigy." Now had he meant to confine the meaning of "miracle" and "prodigy" to a violation of the laws of *matter*, the epithet "*miraculous*," applied, even thus hypothetically, to *false testimony*, would be as unmeaning as the epithets "green," or "square;" the only possible sense in which we can apply to it, even in imagination, the term "miraculous," is that of "highly improbable,"—"contrary to those laws of nature which respect human conduct:" and in this sense accordingly he uses the word in the very next sentence: "When any one tells me that he saw a dead man restored to life, I immediately

this additional circumstance which renders the contradiction of experience more glaring in this case than in that of the miraculous histories which ingenious sceptics have held up to contempt: all the advocates of miracles admit that they are rare exceptions to the general course of nature, but contend that they must needs be so, on account of the rarity of those extraordinary *occasions* which are the *reason* of their being performed : a miracle, they say, does not happen every day, because a revelation is not given every day It would be foreign to the present purpose to seek for arguments against this answer : I leave it to those who are engaged in the controversy, to find a reply to it ; but my present object is to point out that this solution does not at all apply in the present case. Where is the peculiarity of the *occasion ?* What sufficient *reason* is there for a series of events occurring in the eighteenth and nineteenth centuries, which never took place before ?

consider with myself whether it be more *probable* that this person should either deceive or be deceived, or that the fact which he relates should really have happened. I weigh the one *miracle* against the other."—Hume's " Essay on Miracles," pp. 176, 177, 12mo; p. 182, 8vo, 1767 ; p. 115, 8vo, 1817.

See also a passage above quoted from the same essay, where he speaks of "the *miraculous* accounts of travellers," evidently using the word in this sense. Perhaps it was superfluous to cite authority for applying the term "miracle" to whatever is highly "improbable ;" but it is important to the students of Hume, to be fully aware that *he* uses those two expressions as synonymous; since otherwise they would mistake the meaning of that passage which he justly calls " a general maxim worthy of our attention."

Was Europe at that period peculiarly weak, and in a state of barbarism, that one man could achieve such conquests, and acquire such a vast empire? On the contrary, she was flourishing in the height of strength and civilization. Can the persevering attachment and blind devotedness of the French to this man be accounted for by his being the descendant of a long line of kings, whose race was hallowed by hereditary veneration? No; we are told he was a low-born usurper, and not even a Frenchman! Is it that he was a good and kind sovereign? He is represented not only as an imperious and merciless despot, but as most wantonly careless of the lives of his soldiers. Could the French army and people have failed to hear from the wretched survivors of his supposed Russian expedition, how they had left the corpses of above 100,000 of their comrades bleaching on the snow-drifts of that dismal country, whither his mad ambition had conducted them, and where his selfish cowardice had deserted them? Wherever we turn to seek for circumstances that may help to account for the events of this incredible story, we only meet with such as aggravate its improbability.* Had it been told of some distant

---

* "Events may be so extraordinary that they can hardly be established by testimony. We would not give credit to a man who would affirm that he saw an hundred dice thrown in the air, and that they all fell on the same faces."—*Edinburgh Review*, Sept. 1814, p. 327.

Let it be observed that the instance here given is *miraculous* in no other sense but that of being highly *improbable*.

country, at a remote period, we could not have told what peculiar circumstances there might have been to render probable what seems to us most strange; and yet in *that* case every philosophical sceptic, every free-thinking speculator, would instantly have rejected such a history, as utterly unworthy of credit. What, for instance, would the great Hume, or any of the philosophers of his school have said, if they had found in the antique records of any nation such a passage as this: "There was a certain man of Corsica, whose name was Napoleon, and he was one of the chief captains of the host of the French; and he gathered together an army, and went and fought against Egypt; but when the King of Britain heard thereof, he sent ships of war and valiant men to fight against the French in Egypt. So they warred against them, and prevailed, and strengthened the hands of the rulers of the land against the French, and drave away Napoleon from before the city of Acre. Then Napoleon left the captains and the army that were in Egypt, and fled, and returned back to France. So the French people took Napoleon, and made him ruler over them, and he became exceeding great, insomuch that there was none like him of all that had ruled over France before."

What, I say, would Hume have thought of this, especially if he had been told that it was at this day generally credited? Would he not have confessed that he had been mistaken in supposing there was a peculiarly blind credulity and prejudice in favour of everything that is accounted *sacred;** for that, since even professed sceptics swallow implicitly such a story as this, it appears there must be a still blinder prejudice in favour of everything that is *not* accounted sacred?

Suppose again we found in this history such passages as the following: "And it came to pass after these things that Napoleon strengthened himself, and gathered together another host instead of that which he had lost, and went and warred against the Prussians, and the Russians, and the Austrians, and all the rulers of the north country, which were confederate against him. And the ruler of Sweden also, which was a Frenchman, warred against Napoleon. So they went forth, and fought against the French in the plain of Leipsic. And the French were discomfited before their enemies, and fled, and came to the rivers which are behind Leipsic, and essayed to pass over, that they might escape out of the hand of their enemies; but they could not, for Napoleon had broken down the

---

* "If the spirit of religion join itself to the love of wonder, there is an end of common sense; and human testimony in these circumstances loses all pretensions to authority."—Hume's "Essay on Miracles," p. 179, 12mo; p. 185, 8vo, 1767; p. 117, 8vo, 1817.

bridges; so the people of the north countries came upon them, and smote them with a very grievous slaughter." .... .

"Then the ruler of Austria and all the rulers of the north countries sent messengers unto Napoleon to speak peaceably unto him, saying, Why should there be war between us any more? Now Napoleon had put away his wife, and taken the daughter of the ruler of Austria to wife. So all the counsellors of Napoleon came and stood before him, and said, Behold now these kings are merciful kings; do even as they say unto thee; knowest thou not yet that France is destroyed? But he spake roughly unto his counsellors, and drave them out from his presence, neither would he hearken unto their voice. And when all the kings saw that, they warred against France, and smote it with the edge of the sword, and came near to Paris, which is the royal city, to take it: so the men of Paris went out, and delivered up the city to them. Then those kings spake kindly unto the men of Paris, saying, Be of good cheer, there shall no harm happen unto you. Then were the men of Paris glad, and said, Napoleon is a tyrant; he shall no more rule over us. Also all the princes, the judges, the counsellors, and the captains, whom Napoleon had raised up, even from the lowest of the people, sent unto Louis, the brother of King Louis whom they had slain, and made him king over France." ....

"And when Napoleon saw that the kingdom was departed from him, he said unto the rulers which came against him, Let me, I pray you, give the kingdom unto my son; but they would not hearken unto him. Then he spake yet again, saying, Let me, I pray you, go and live in the island of Elba, which is over against Italy, nigh unto the coast of France; and ye shall give me an allowance for me and my household, and the land of Elba also for a possession. So they made him ruler of Elba." . . . .

"In those days the Pope returned unto his own land. Now the French, and divers other nations of Europe, are servants of the Pope, and hold him in reverence; but he is an abomination unto the Britons, and to the Prussians, and to the Russians, and to the Swedes. Howbeit the French had taken away all his lands, and robbed him of all that he had, and carried him away captive into France. But when the Britons, and the Prussians, and the Russians, and the Swedes, and the rest of the nations that were confederate against France, came thither, they caused the French to set the Pope at liberty, and to restore all his goods that they had taken; likewise, they gave him back all his possessions; and he went home in peace, and ruled over his own city as in times past." . . . .

"And it came to pass when Napoleon had not yet been a full year in Elba, that he said unto his men of war which clave unto him, Go to, let us go back to France, and fight against King Louis, and thrust him out from being king. So he departed, he and 600 men with him that drew the sword, and warred against King Louis. Then all the men of Belial gathered themselves together, and said, God save Napoleon. And when Louis saw that, he fled, and gat him into the land of Batavia ; and Napoleon ruled over France," &c. &c. &c.

Now if a freethinking philosopher—one of those who advocate the cause of unbiassed reason, and despised pretended revelations—were to meet with such a tissue of absurdities as this in an old Jewish record, would he not reject it at once as too palpable an imposture* to deserve even any inquiry into its evidence? Is that credible then of the civilized Europeans now which could not, if reported of the semi-barbarous Jews 3000 years ago, be established by any testimony? Will it be answered that "there is nothing *supernatural* in all this?" Why is it, then, that you object to what is *supernatural*—that you reject every account of *miracles*—if not *because* they are *improbable?* Surely,

---

* "I desire any one to lay his hand upon his heart, and after serious consideration declare whether he thinks that the falsehood of such a book, supported by such testimony, would be more extraordinary and miraculous than all the miracles it relates."—Hume's "Essay on Miracles," p. 200, 12mo ; p. 206, 8vo, 1767 ; p. 131, 8vo, 1817.

Let it be borne in mind that Hume (as I have above remarked) continually employs the terms "miracle" and "prodigy" to signify any thing that is highly *improbable* and *extraordinary.*

then, a story equally or still more improbable, is not to be implicitly received, merely on the ground that it is *not* miraculous: though in fact, as I have already (in note p. 275) shown from Hume's authority, it really *is* miraculous. The opposition to experience has been proved to be as complete in this case as in what are commonly called miracles; and the reasons assigned for that contrariety by the defenders of *them* cannot be pleaded in the present instance. If, then, philosophers, who reject every wonderful story that is maintained by priests, are yet found ready to believe *everything else*, however improbable, they will surely lay themselves open to the accusation brought against them of being unduly prejudiced against whatever relates to religion.

There is one more circumstance which I cannot forbear mentioning, because it so much adds to the air of fiction which pervades every part of this marvellous tale; and that is, the *nationality* of it.*

Buonaparte prevailed over all the hostile States in turn, *except England;* in the zenith of his power his fleets were swept from the sea, *by England;* his troops always defeat an equal, and frequently even a superior, number of those of any other nation,

---

* "The wise lend a very academic faith to every report which favours the passion of the reporter, whether it magnifies his *country*, his family, or himself."—Hume's "Essay on Miracles;" p. 144, 12mo; p. 200, 8vo, 1767; p. 126, 8vo, 1817.

except the English, and with them it is just the reverse; twice, and twice only, he is personally engaged against an *English commander*, and both times he is totally defeated, at Acre and at Waterloo; and, to crown all, *England* finally crushes this tremendous power, which has so long kept the Continent in subjection or in alarm, and to the *English* he surrenders himself prisoner! Thoroughly national to be sure! It *may* be all very true; but I would only ask, *if* a story *had* been fabricated for the express purpose of amusing the English nation, could it have been contrived more ingeniously? It would do admirably for an epic poem; and indeed bears a considerable resemblance to the Iliad and the Æneid, in which Achilles and the Greeks, Æneas and the Trojans (the ancestors of the Romans), are so studiously held up to admiration. Buonaparte's exploits seem magnified in order to enhance the glory of his conquerors, just as Hector is allowed to triumph during the absence of Achilles merely to give additional splendour to his overthrow by the arm of that invincible hero. Would not this circumstance alone render a history rather *suspicious* in the eyes of an acute critic, even if it were not filled with such gross improbabilities; and induce him to suspend his judgment, till very satisfactory evidence (far stronger than can be found in this case) should be produced.

Is it then too much to demand of the wary

academic * a suspension of judgment as to the "life and adventures of Napoleon Buonaparte?" I do not pretend to *decide* positively that there is not, nor ever was, any such person; but merely to propose it as a *doubtful* point, and one the more deserving of careful investigation from the very circumstance of its having hitherto been admitted without inquiry. Far less would I undertake to decide what is, or has been, the real state of affairs: he who points out the improbability of the current story is not bound to suggest an hypothesis of his own †—though it may safely be affirmed that it would be hard to invent any more improbable than the received one. One may surely be allowed to hesitate in admitting the stories which the ancient poets tell, of earthquakes and volcanic eruptions being caused by imprisoned giants, without being called upon satisfactorily to account for those phenomena.

Amidst the defect of valid evidence under which, as I have already shown, we labour in the present instance, it is hardly possible to offer more than here and there a probable conjecture; or to pronounce how much may be true, and how much

* "Nothing can be more contrary than such a philosophy" (the academic or sceptical) "to the supine indolence of the mind, its rash arrogance, its lofty pretensions, and its superstitious credulity."—Fifth Essay, p. 68, 12mo; p. 41, 8vo, 1817.

† See Hume's "Essay on Miracles," pp. 189, 191, 195, 12mo; pp. 193, 197, 201, 202, 8vo, 1767; pp. 124, 125, 126, 8vo, 1817.

fictitious, in the accounts presented to us; for it is to be observed that this case is much *more* open to sceptical doubts even than some miraculous histories, for some of them are of such a nature that you cannot consistently admit a part and reject the rest, but are bound, if you are satisfied as to the reality of any one miracle, to embrace the whole system, so that it is necessary for the sceptic to impeach the evidence of *all* of them, separately and collectively: whereas *here*, each single point requires to be *established* separately, since no one of them authenticates the rest. Supposing there be a State prisoner at St. Helena (which, by the way, it is acknowleged many of the French disbelieve), how do we know who he is, or why he is confined there? There have been State prisoners before now, who were never guilty of subjugating half Europe, and whose offences have been very imperfectly ascertained. Admitting that there have been bloody wars going on for several years past, which is highly probable, it does not follow that the events of those wars were such as we have been told—that Buonaparte was the author and conductor of them, or that such a person ever existed. What disturbances may have taken place in the government of the French people, we, and even nineteen-twentieths of *them*, have no means of learning but from imperfect hearsay evidence; but that there have been numerous bloody wars with France under the dominion of the *Bourbons* we are well assured : and we are now told that France is governed by a Bourbon king of the name of Louis, who professes to be in the twenty-third year of his reign. Let every one conjecture for himself. I am far from pretending to decide who may have been the governor or governors of the French nation, and the leaders of their armies, for several years past. Certain it is, that when men are indulging their inclination for the marvellous, they always show a strong propensity to accumulate upon one individual (real or imaginary) the exploits of many, besides multiplying and exaggerating these exploits a thousandfold. Thus, the expounders of the ancient mythology tell us there were several persons of the name of Hercules (either originally bearing that appellation, or having it applied to them as an honour), whose collective feats, after being dressed up in a sufficiently marvellous garb, were attributed to a single hero. Is it not just possible, that during the rage for words of Greek derivation, the title of "Napoleon" (Ναπολεων), which signifies "Lion of the Forest," may have been conferred by the popular voice on more than one favourite general, distinguished for irresistible valour? Is it not also possible that "Buona parte" may have been originally a sort of cant term applied to the "good (*i.e.*, the bravest or most patriotic) part" of the French army collectively, and have been afterwards mistaken for the proper name of an individual? I do not profess to support this conjecture; but it is certain that such mistakes may and do occur. Some critics have supposed that the Athenians imagined Anastasis ("Resurrection") to be a new goddess, in whose cause Paul was preaching. Would it have been thought anything incredible if we had been told that the ancient Persians, who had no idea of any but a monarchical government, had supposed Aristocratia to be a Queen of Sparta? But we need not confine ourselves to hypothetical cases: it is positively stated that the Hindoos at this day believe "the Honourable East India Company" to be a venerable old lady of high dignity, residing in this country. The Germans of the present day derive their name from a similar mistake. The first tribe of them who invaded Gaul* assumed the honourable title of "*Ger-man*," which signifies "warrior"—(the words "war" and "guerre," as well as "man," which remains in our language unaltered, are evidently derived from the Teutonic)—and the Gauls applied this as a *name* to the whole race.

However, I merely throw out these conjectures without by any means contending that more plausible ones might not be suggested. But what-

* "Germaniæ vocabulum recens et nuper additum; quoniam, qui primi Rhenum transgressi Gallos expulerint, ac nunc Tungri, tunc Germani vocati sint: ita nationis nomen in nomen gentis evaluisse paullatim, ut omnes, primum a victore ob metum, mox a seipsis invento nomine, Germani vocarentur."—Tacitus, "De Mor. Germ."

ever supposition we adopt, or whether we adopt any, the objections to the commonly received accounts will remain in their full force, and imperiously demand the attention of the candid sceptic.

I call upon those, therefore, who profess themselves advocates of free inquiry—who disdain to be carried along with the stream of popular opinion, and who will listen to no testimony that runs counter to experience—to follow up their own principles fairly and consistently. Let the same mode of argument be adopted in all cases alike; and then it can no longer be attributed to hostile prejudice, but to enlarged and philosophical views. If they have already rejected some histories, on the ground of their being strange and marvellous—of their relating facts unprecedented and at variance with the established course of nature—let them not give credit to another history which lies open to the very same objections, the extraordinary and romantic tale we have been just considering. If they have discredited the testimony of witnesses, who are *said* at least to have been disinterested, and to have braved persecutions and death in support of their assertions, can these philosophers consistently listen to and believe the testimony of those who avowedly *get money* by the tales they publish, and who do not even pretend that they incur any serious risk in case of being detected in a falsehood? If in other cases they have refused to listen to an account which has passed

K

through many intermediate hands before it reaches them, and which is defended by those who have an interest in maintaining it ; let them consider through how many and what very suspicious hands *this* story has arrived to them, without the possibility (as I have shown) of tracing it back to any decidedly authentic source, after all ;* and likewise how strong an interest, in every way, those who have hitherto imposed on them have in keeping up the imposture : let them, in short, show themselves as ready to detect the cheats and despise the fables of politicians as of priests. But if they are still wedded to the popular belief in this point, let them be consistent enough to admit the same evidence in *other* cases which they yield to in *this*. If, after all that has been said, they cannot bring themselves to doubt of the existence of Napoleon Buonaparte, they must at least acknowledge that they do not apply to that question the same plan of reasoning which they have made use of in others ; and they are consequently bound in reason and in honesty to renounce it altogether.

* For let it not be forgotten, that these writers *themselves refer* to no better authority than that of an *unnamed and unknown* foreign correspondent.

ADVICE

TO A

YOUNG REVIEWER,

WITH A

SPECIMEN OF THE ART.

Advice to a Young Reviewer.

You are now about to enter on a profession which has the means of doing much good to society, and scarcely any temptation to do harm. You may encourage genius, you may chastise superficial arrogance, expose falsehood, correct error, and guide the taste and opinions of the age in no small degree by the books you praise and recommend. All this too may be done without running the risk of making any enemies, or subjecting yourself to be called to account for your criticism, however severe. While your name is unknown, your person is invulnerable: at the same time your own aim is sure, for you may take it at your leisure; and your blows fall heavier than those of any writer whose name is given, or who is simply anonymous. There is a mysterious authority in the plural *we*, which no single name, whatever may be its reputation, can acquire; and under the sanction of this imposing style your strictures, your praises, and your dogmas will command universal attention, and be received as the fruit of united talents, acting on one common principle—as the judgments of a tribunal who decide only on mature deliberation, and who protect the interests of literature with unceasing vigilance.

Such being the high importance of that office, and such its opportunities, I cannot bestow a few hours of leisure better than in furnishing you with some hints for the more easy and effectual discharge of it: hints which are, I confess, loosely thrown together, but which are the result of long experience, and of frequent reflection and comparison. And if anything should strike you at first sight as rather equivocal in point of morality, or deficient in liberality and feeling, I beg you will suppress all such scruples, and consider them as the offspring of a contracted education and narrow way of thinking, which a little intercourse with the world and sober reasoning will speedily overcome.

Now, as in the conduct of life nothing is more to be desired than some governing principle of action, to which all other principles and motives must be made subservient, so in the art of reviewing I would lay down as a fundamental position, which you must never lose sight of, and which must be the mainspring of all your criticisms—*write what will sell.* To this golden rule every minor canon must be subordinate, and must be either immediately deducible from it, or at least be made consistent with it. Be not staggered at the sound of a precept, which upon examination will be found as honest and virtuous as it is discreet. I have already sketched out the great services which it is in your power to render mankind; but all your efforts would be unavailing if men did not read what you write. Your utility therefore, it is plain, depends upon your popularity; and popularity cannot be attained without humouring the taste and inclinations of men.

Be assured that by a similar train of sound and judicious reasoning the consciences of thousands in public life are daily quieted. It is better for the State that their party should govern than any other: the good which they can effect by the exercise of power is infinitely greater than any which could arise from a rigid adherence to certain subordinate moral precepts, which therefore should be violated without scruple whenever they stand in the way of their leading purpose. He who sticks at these can never act a great part in the world, and is not fit to act it if he could. Such maxims may be very useful in ordinary affairs, and for the guidance of ordinary men; but when we mount into the sphere of public utility, we must adopt more enlarged principles, and not suffer ourselves to be cramped and fettered by petty notions of right and moral duty.

When you have reconciled yourself to this liberal way of thinking, you will find many inferior advantages resulting from it, which at first did not enter into your consideration. In particular, it will greatly lighten your labours to *follow* the public taste, instead of taking upon you to *direct* it. The task of pleasing is at all times easier than that of instructing: at least it does not stand in need of painful research and preparation, and may be effected in general by a little vivacity of manner, and a dexterous morigeration (as Lord Bacon calls it) to the humours and frailties of men. Your responsibility, too, is thereby much lessened. Justice and candour can only be required of you so far as they coincide with this main principle; and a little experience will convince you that these are not the happiest means of accomplishing your purpose.

It has been idly said, that a Reviewer acts in a judicial capacity, and that his conduct should be regulated by the same rules by which the Judge of a civil court is governed: that he should rid himself of every bias; be patient, cautious, sedate, and rigidly impartial; that he should not seek to show off himself, and should check every disposition to enter into the case as a partisan.

Such is the language of superficial thinkers; but in reality there is no analogy between the two cases. A Judge is promoted to that office by the authority of the State; a Reviewer by his own. The former is independent of control, and may therefore freely follow the dictates of his own conscience; the latter depends for his very bread upon the breath of public opinion: the great law of self-preservation therefore points out to him a different line of action. Besides, as we have already observed, if he ceases to please he is no longer read, and consequently is no longer useful. In a court of justice, too, the part of amusing the bystanders rests with the counsel: in the case of criticism, if the Reviewer himself does not undertake it, who will? Instead of vainly aspiring therefore to the gravity of a magistrate, I would advise him, when he sits down to write, to place himself in the imaginary situation of a cross-examining pleader. He may comment, in a vein of agreeable irony, upon the profession, the manner of life, the look, dress, or even the name of the witness he is examining: when he has raised a contemptuous opinion of him in the minds of the court, he may proceed to draw answers from him capable of a ludicrous turn, and he may carve and garble these to his own liking. This mode of proceeding you will find most practicable in poetry, where the boldness of the image, or the delicacy of thought, for which the reader's mind was prepared in the original, will easily be made to appear extravagant or affected, if judiciously singled out and detached from the group to which it belongs. Again, since much depends upon the rhythm and the terseness of expression, both of which are sometimes destroyed by dropping a single word, or transposing a phrase, I have known much advantage arise from not quoting in the form of a literal extract, but giving a brief summary in prose of the contents of a poetical passage; and interlarding your own language with occasional phrases of the poem, marked with inverted commas. These, and a thousand other little expedients, by which the arts of quizzing and banter flourish, practice will soon teach you. If it should be necessary to transcribe a dull passage, not very fertile in topics of humour and raillery, you may introduce it as a "favourable specimen of the author's manner."

Few people are aware of the powerful effects of what is philosophically termed association. Without any positive violation of truth, the whole dignity of a passage may be undermined by contriving to raise some vulgar and ridiculous notions in the mind of the reader; and language teems with examples of words by which the same idea is expressed, with the difference only that one excites a feeling of respect, the other of contempt. Thus, you may call a fit of melancholy "the sulks," resentment "a pet," a steed "a nag," a feast "a junketing," sorrow and affliction "whining and blubbering." By transferring the terms peculiar to one state of society to analogous situations and characters in another, the same object is attained, a drill-sergeant or a cat-and-nine-tails in the Trojan War, a Lesbos smack put in to the Piræus, the penny-post of Jerusalem, and other combinations of the like nature, which, when you have a little indulged that vein of thought, will readily suggest themselves, never fail to raise a smile, if not immediately at the expense of the author, yet entirely destructive of that frame of mind which his poem requires in order to be relished.

I have dwelt the longer on this branch of literature, because you are chiefly to look here for materials of fun and irony. Voyages and travels indeed are no barren ground, and you must seldom let a number of your Review go abroad without an article of this description. The charm of this species of writing, so universally felt, arises chiefly from its uniting narrative with information. The interest we take in the story can only be kept alive by minute incident and occasional detail, which puts us in possession of the traveller's feelings, his hopes, his fears, his disappointments, and his pleasures. At the same time the thirst for knowledge and love of novelty is gratified by continual information respecting the people and countries he visits. If you wish, therefore, to run down the book, you have only to play off these two parts against each other: when the writer's object is to satisfy the first inclination, you are to thank him for communicating to the world such valuable facts—as whether he lost his way in the night—or sprained his ankle—or had no appetite to his dinner. If he is busied about describing the mineralogy, natural history, agriculture, trade, &c., of a country, you may mention a hundred books from whence the same information may be obtained, and deprecate the practice of emptying old musty folios into new quartos, to gratify that sickly taste for a smattering about everything which distinguishes the present age.

In works of science and recondite learning, the task you have undertaken will not be so difficult as you may imagine. Tables of contents and indexes are blessed helps in the hands of a Reviewer; but, more than all, the preface is the field from which his richest harvest is to be gathered. In the preface the author usually gives a summary of what has been written on the same subject before; he acknowledges the assistance he has received from different sources, and the reasons of his dissent from former writers; he confesses that certain parts have been less attentively considered than others, and that information has come to his hands too late to be made use of; he points out many things in the composition of his work which he thinks may provoke animadversion, and endeavours to defend or to palliate his own practice. Here then is a fund of wealth for the Reviewer, lying upon the very surface; if he knows anything of his business, he will turn all these materials against the author, carefully suppressing the source of his information, and as if drawing from the stores of his own mind, long ago laid up for this very purpose. If the author's references are correct, a great point is gained; for, by consulting a few passages of the original works, it will be easy to discuss the subject with the air of having a previous knowledge of the whole. Your chief vantage-ground is that you may fasten upon any position in the book you are reviewing, and treat it as principal and essential, when perhaps it is of little weight in the main argument; but, by allotting a large share of your criticism to it, the reader will naturally be led to give it a proportionate importance, and to consider the merit of the treatise at issue upon that single question. If anybody complains that the greater and more valuable parts remain unnoticed, your answer is that it is impossible to pay attention to all, and that your duty is rather to prevent the propagation of error than to lavish praises upon that which, if really excellent, will work its way in the world without your help. Indeed, if the plan of your Review admits of selection, you had better not meddle with works of deep research and original speculation, such as have already attracted much notice, and cannot be treated superficially without fear of being found out. The time required for making yourself thoroughly master of the subject is so great, that you may depend upon it they will never pay for the reviewing. They are generally the fruit of long study, and of talents concentrated in the steady pursuit of one object; it is not likely therefore that you can throw much new light on a question of this nature, or even plausibly combat the author's positions in the course of a few hours, which is all you can well afford to devote to them. And, without accomplishing one or other of these points, your review will gain no celebrity, and of course no good will be done.

Enough has been said to give you some insight into the facilities with which your new employment abounds: I will only mention one more, because of its extensive and almost universal application to all branches of literature—the topic, I mean, which by the old Rhetoricians was called ἐξ ἐναντίων. That is, when a work excels in one quality, you may blame it for not having the opposite. For instance, if the biographical sketch of a literary character is minute and full of anecdote, you may enlarge on the advantages of philosophical reflection, and the superior mind required to give a judicious analysis of the opinions and works of deceased authors; on the contrary, if the latter method is pursued by the biographer, you can with equal ease extol the lively colouring and truth and interest of exact delineation and detail. This topic, you will perceive, enters into style as well as matter, where many virtues might be named which are incompatible; and, whichever the author has preferred, it will be the signal for you to launch forth on the praises of its opposite, and continually to hold up that to your reader as the model of excellence in this species of writing.

You will, perhaps, wonder why all my instructions are pointed towards the censure and not the praise of books; but many reasons might be given why it should be so. The chief are, that this part is both easier, and will sell better. Let us hear the words of Mr. Burke on a subject not very dissimilar: "In such cases," says he, "the writer has a certain fire and alacrity inspired into him by a consciousness that, let it fare how it will with the subject, his ingenuity will be sure of applause; and this alacrity becomes much greater, if he acts upon the offensive, by the impetuosity that always accompanies an attack, and the unfortunate propensity which mankind have to the finding and exaggerating faults." (Pref. Vindic. Nat. Soc., p. 6.) You will perceive that I have on no occasion sanctioned the baser motives of private pique, envy, revenge, and love of detraction; at least, I have not recommended harsh treatment upon any of these grounds; I have argued simply on the abstract moral principle which a Reviewer should ever have present to his mind: but if any of these motives insinuate themselves as secondary springs of action, I would not condemn them; they may come in aid of the grand leading principle, and powerfully second its operation.

But it is time to close these tedious precepts, and

to furnish you with what speaks plainer than any precept, a specimen of the art itself, in which several of them are embodied. It is hastily done, but it exemplifies well enough what I have said of the poetical department, and exhibits most of those qualities which disappointed authors are fond of railing at, under the names of flippancy, arrogance, conceit, misrepresentation, and malevolence; reproaches which you will only regard as so many acknowledgments of success in your undertaking, and infallible tests of an established fame and rapidly increasing circulation.

L'Allegro: a Poem. By JOHN MILTON. No Printer's name.

IT has become a practice of late with a certain description of people, who have no visible means of subsistence, to string together a few trite images of rural scenery, interspersed with vulgarisms in dialect and traits of vulgar manners; to dress up these materials in a sing-song jingle, and to offer them for sale as a poem. According to the most approved recipes, something about the heathen gods and goddesses, and the schoolboy topics of Styx, and Cerberus, and Elysium, is occasionally thrown in, and the composition is complete. The stock-in-trade of these adventurers is in general scanty enough, and their art therefore consists in disposing it to the best advantage. But if such be the aim of the writer, it is the critic's business to detect and defeat the imposture; to warn the public against the purchase of shop-worn goods and tinsel wares; to protect the fair trader, by exposing the tricks of needy quacks and mountebanks; and to chastise that forward and noisy importunity with which they present themselves to the public notice.

How far Mr. Milton is amenable to this discipline will best appear from a brief analysis of the poem before us. In the very opening he assumes a tone of authority, which might better suit some veteran bard than a raw candidate for the Delphic bays: for, before he proceeds to the regular process of invocation, he clears the way by driving from his presence, with sundry hard names and bitter reproaches on her father, mother, and all the family, a venerable personage, whose age at least, and staid matron-like appearance, might have entitled her to more civil language.

> Hence, loathed Melancholy;
> Of Cerberus and blackest midnight born,
> In Stygian cave forlorn, &c.

There is no giving rules, however, in these matters, without a knowledge of the case. Perhaps the old lady had been frequently warned off before, and provoked this violence by continuing still to lurk about the poet's dwelling. And, to say the truth, the reader will have but too good reason to remark, before he gets through the poem, that it is one thing to tell the spirit of dulness to depart, and another to get rid of her in reality. Like Glendower's spirits, any one may order them away, "but will they go when you do order them?"

But let us suppose for a moment that the Parnassian decree is obeyed, and according to the letter of the *order*, which is as precise and wordy as if Justice Shallow himself had drawn it, that the obnoxious female is sent back to the place of her birth,

> 'Mongst horrid shapes, shrieks, sights, &c.,

at which we beg our fair readers not to be alarmed, for we can assure them they are only words of course in all poetical instruments of this nature, and mean no more than the "force and arms," and "instigation of the devil" in a common indictment. This nuisance then being abated, we are left at liberty to contemplate a character of a different complexion, "buxom, blithe, and debonair," one who, although evidently a great favourite of the poet's, and therefore to be received with all due courtesy, is notwithstanding introduced under the suspicious description of an *alias:*

> In heaven ycleped Euphrosyne,
> And by men, heart-easing Mirth.

Judging indeed from the light and easy deportment of this gay nymph, one might guess there were good reasons for a change of name as she changed her residence.

But of all vices there is none we abhor more than that of slanderous insinuation; we shall, therefore, confine our moral strictures to the nymph's mother, in whose defence the poet has little to say himself. Here too, as in the case of the *name*, there is some doubt: for the uncertainty of descent on the father's side having become trite to a proverb, the author, scorning that beaten track, has left us to choose between two mothers for his favourite, and without much to guide our choice; for, whichever we fix upon, it is plain she was no better than she should be. As he seems, however, himself inclined to the latter of the two, we will even suppose it so to be:

>Or whether (as some sager sing)
>The frolic *wind that breathes the spring*,
>Zephyr with Aurora playing,
>*As he met her once a-Maying;*
>There on beds of violets blue,
>And fresh-blown roses washed in dew, &c.

Some dull people might imagine that the wind was more like the breath of spring, than spring the breath of the wind; but we are more disposed to question the author's ethics than his physics, and accordingly cannot dismiss these May gambols without some observations.

In the first place, Mr. M. seems to have higher notions of the antiquity of the Maypole than we have been accustomed to attach to it. Or perhaps he thought to shelter the equivocal nature of this affair under that sanction. To us however, who can hardly subscribe to the doctrine that "vice loses half its evil by losing all its grossness," neither the remoteness of time nor the gaiety of the season furnishes a sufficient palliation. "Violets blue" and "fresh-blown roses" are, to be sure, more agreeable objects of the imagination than a ginshop in Wapping or a booth in Bartholomew Fair; but in point of morality these are distinctions without a difference; or, it may be, the cultivation of mind, which teaches us to reject and nauseate these latter objects, aggravates the case if our improvement in taste be not accompanied by a proportionate improvement of morals.

If the reader can reconcile himself to this latitude of principle, the anachronism will not long stand in his way. Much, indeed, may be said in favour of this union of ancient mythology with modern notions and manners. It is a sort of chronological metaphor—an artificial analogy, by which ideas, widely remote and heterogeneous, are brought into contact, and the mind is delighted by this unexpected assemblage, as it is by the combinations of figurative language.

Thus in that elegant interlude, which the pen of Ben Jonson has transmitted to us, of the loves of Hero and Leander:

> Gentles, that no longer your expectations may wander,
> Behold our chief actor, amorous Leander,
> With a great deal of cloth, lapped about him like a scarf,
> For he yet serves his father, a dyer in Puddle Wharf;
> Which place we'll make bold with, to call it our Abydus,
> As the Bank side is our Sestos, and *let it not be denied us.*

And far be it from us to deny the use of so reasonable a liberty; especially if the request be backed (as it is in the case of Mr. M.) by the craving and imperious necessities of rhyme. What man who has ever bestrode Pegasus but for an hour, will be insensible to such a claim?

> Haud ignara mali miseris succurrere disco.

We are next favoured with an enumeration of the attendants of this "debonair" nymph, in all the minuteness of a German dramatis personæ, or a rope-dancer's handbill:

> Haste thee, nymph, and bring with thee
> Jest, and youthful Jollity;
> Quips, and cranks, and wanton wiles,
> Nods, and becks, and wreathèd smiles,
> Such as hang on Hebe's cheek,
> And love to live in dimple sleek;
> Sport that wrinkled Care derides,
> And Laughter, holding both his sides.

The author, to prove himself worthy of being admitted of the crew, skips and capers about upon "the light fantastic toe," that there is no following him. He scampers through all the categories, in search of his imaginary beings, from substance to quality, and back again; from thence to action, passion, habit, &c., with incredible celerity. Who, for instance, would have expected *cranks, nods, becks,* and *wreathèd smiles* as part of a group, in which Jest, Jollity, Sport and Laughter figure away as full-formed entire personages? The family likeness is certainly very strong in the two last, and if we had not been told we should perhaps have thought the act of *deriding* as appropriate to laughter as to sport.

But how are we to understand the stage directions?

> *Come,* and trip it as you *go.*

Are the words used synonymously? Or is it meant that this airy gentry shall come in at a minuet step, and go off in a jig? The phenomenon of a *tripping crank* is indeed novel, and would doubtless attract numerous spectators. But it is difficult to guess to whom among this jolly company the poet addresses himself, for immediately after the plural appellative [you], he proceeds:

> And in *thy* right hand lead with *thee*
> The mountain nymph, sweet Liberty.

No sooner is this fair damsel introduced, but Mr. M., with most unbecoming levity, falls in love with her, and makes a request of her companion, which is rather greedy, that he may live with both of them:

> To live with her, and live with thee.

Even the gay libertine who sung, "How happy could I be with either," did not go so far as this. But we have already had occasion to remark on the laxity of Mr. M.'s amatory notions.

The poet, intoxicated with the charms of his mistress, now rapidly runs over the pleasures which he proposes to himself in the enjoyment of her society. But though he has the advantage of being his own caterer, either his palate is of a peculiar structure, or he has not made the most judicious selection. To begin the day well, he will have the *skylark*

> to come in *spite of sorrow*,
> And at his window bid good morrow.

The skylark, if we know anything of the nature of that bird, must come in spite of something else as well as of sorrow, to the performance of this office. In his next image the natural history is better preserved, and as the thoughts are appropriate to the time of the day, we will venture to transcribe the passage, as a favourable specimen of the author's manner:

> While the cock with lively din
> Scatters the rear of darkness thin,
> And to the stack, or the barn-door,
> Stoutly struts his dames before;
> Oft listening how the hounds and horn
> Cheerly rouse the slumbering morn,
> From the side of some hoar hill,
> Through the high wood echoing shrill.

Is it not lamentable that, after all, whether it is the cock or the poet that listens, should be left entirely to the reader's conjecture? Perhaps also his embarrassment may be increased by a slight resemblance of character in these two illustrious personages, at least as far as relates to the extent and numbers of their seraglio.

After a *flaming* description of sunrise, on which occasion the clouds attend in their very best liveries, the bill of fare for the day proceeds in the usual manner. Whistling ploughmen, singing milkmaids, and sentimental shepherds are always to be had at a moment's notice, and, if well grouped, serve to fill up the landscape agreeably enough. On this part of the poem we have only to remark, that if Mr. John Milton proposes to make himself merry with

> Russet lawns, and fallows grey,
> Where the nibbling flocks *do* stray;
> Mountains on whose barren breast
> The labouring clouds *do* often rest,
> Meadows trim with daisies pied,
> Shallow brooks, and rivers wide,
> Towers and battlements, &c. &c. &c.,

he will either find himself egregiously disappointed, or he must possess a disposition to merriment which even Democritus himself might envy. To such a pitch indeed does this solemn indication of joy sometimes rise, that we are inclined to give him credit for a literal adherence to the Apostolic precept, "Is any merry, let him sing psalms."

At length, however, he hies away at the sound of bell-ringing, and seems for some time to enjoy the tippling and fiddling and dancing of a village wake; but his fancy is soon haunted again by spectres and goblins, a set of beings not in general esteemed the companions or inspirers of mirth.

> With stories told of many a feat,
> How fairy Mab the junkets eat;
> She was pinched, and pulled, she said;
> And he, by friar's lanthern led,
> Tells how the drudging goblin sweat
> To earn his cream-bowl duly 'set;
> When in one night, ere glimpse of morn,
> His shadowy flail hath threshed the corn,
> That ten day-labourers could not end;
> Then lies him down the lubbar fiend,
> And, stretched out all the chimney's length,
> Basks at the fire his hairy strength;
> And crop-full out of door he flings,
> Ere the first cock his matin rings.

Mr. M. seems indeed to have a turn for this species of nursery tales and prattling lullabies; and if he will studiously cultivate his talent he need not despair of figuring in a conspicuous corner of Mr. Newbury's shop-window; unless indeed Mrs. Trimmer should think fit to proscribe those empty levities and idle superstitions by which the world has been too long abused.

From these rustic fictions we are transported to another species of *hum:*

> Towered cities please us then,
> And the busy hum of men,
> Where throngs of knights and barons bold
> In weeds of peace high triumphs hold,
> With *store of ladies*, whose bright eyes
> *Rain influence*, and judge the prize
> Of wit or arms, while both contend
> To win her grace, whom all commend.

To talk of the bright eyes of ladies judging the prize of wit is indeed with the poets a legitimate species of humming: but would not, we may ask, the *rain* from these ladies' bright eyes rather tend to dim their lustre? Or is there any quality in a shower of *influence*, which, instead of deadening, serves only to brighten and exhilarate? Whatever the case may be, we would advise Mr. M. by all means to keep out of the way of these knights and barons bold; for if he has nothing but his wit to trust to, we will venture to predict that, without a large share of most undue *influence*, he must be content to see the prize adjudged to his competitors.

Of the latter part of the poem little need be said. The author does seem somewhat more at home when he gets among the actors and musicians, though his head is still running upon Orpheus and Eurydice, and Pluto, and other sombre gentry, who are ever thrusting themselves in where we least expect them, and who chill every rising emotion of mirth and gaiety.

He appears, however, to be so ravished with this sketch of festive pleasures, or perhaps with himself for having sketched them so well, that he closes with a couplet, which would not have disgraced a Sternhold:

> These delights if thou canst give,
> Mirth, with thee I *mean* to live.

Of Mr. M.'s good *intentions* there can be no doubt; but we beg leave to remind him that in every compact of this nature there are two opinions to be consulted. He presumes, perhaps, upon the poetical powers he has displayed, and considers them as irresistible; for every one must observe in how different a strain he avows his attachment now and at the opening of the poem. Then it was,

> If I give thee honour due,
> Mirth, admit me of thy crew.

But having, it should seem, established his pretensions, he now thinks it sufficient to give notice that he means to live with her, because he likes her.

Upon the whole, Mr. Milton seems to be possessed of some fancy and talent for rhyming; two most dangerous endowments, which often unfit men for acting a useful part in life, without qualifying them for that which is great and brilliant. If it be true, as we have heard, that he has declined advantageous prospects in business for the sake of indulging his poetical humour, we hope it is not yet too late to prevail upon him to retract his resolution. With the help of Cocker and common industry he may become a respectable scrivener; but it is not all the Zephyrs, and Auroras, and Corydons, and Thyrsises, aye, nor his junketing Queen Mab and drudging goblins, that will ever make him a poet.

GEORGE ROUTLEDGE & SONS' CATALOGUE.

NATURAL HISTORY—ZOOLOGY.

Routledge's Illustrated Natural History. By the Rev. J. G. WOOD, M.A. With more than 1500 Illustrations by COLEMAN, WOLF, HARRISON WEIR, WOOD, ZWECKER, and others. Three Vols., super-royal, cloth, price £2 2s. The Volumes are also sold separately, viz.:—Mammalia, with 600 Illustrations, 14s.; Birds, with 500 Illustrations, 14s.; Reptiles Fishes, and Insects, 400 Illustrations, 14s.

Routledge's Illustrated History of Man. Being an Account of the Manners and Customs of the Uncivilised Races of Men. By the Rev. J. G. WOOD, M.A., F.L.S. With more than 600 Original Illustrations by ZWECKER, DANBY, ANGAS, HANDLEY, and others, engraved by the Brothers DALZIEL. Vol. I., Africa, 14s.; Vol. II., Australia, New Zealand, Polynesia, America, Asia, and Ancient Europe, 14s. Two Vols., super-royal 8vo, cloth, 28s.

The Imperial Natural History. By the Rev. J. G. WOOD. 1000 pages, with 500 Plates, super-royal 8vo, cloth, 15s.

An Illustrated Natural History. By the Rev. J. G. WOOD. With 500 Illustrations by WILLIAM HARVEY, and 8 full-page Plates by WOLF and HARRISON WEIR. Post 8vo, cloth, gilt edges, 6s.

A Picture Natural History. Adapted for Young Readers. By the Rev. J. G. WOOD. With 700 Illustrations by WOLF, WEIR, &c. 4to, cloth, gilt edges, 7s. 6d.

The Popular Natural History. By the Rev. J. G. WOOD. With Hundreds of Illustrations, price 7s. 6d.

The Boy's Own Natural History. By the Rev. J. G. WOOD. With 400 Illustrations, 3s. 6d. cloth.

Sketches and Anecdotes of Animal Life. By the Rev. J. G. WOOD. Illustrated by HARRISON WEIR. Fcap. 8vo, cloth, 3s. 6d.

Animal Traits and Characteristics. By the Rev. J. G. WOOD. Illustrated by H. WEIR. Fcap., cloth, 3s. 6d.

The Poultry Book. By W. B. TEGETMEIER, F.Z.S. Assisted by many Eminent Authorities. With 30 full-page Illustrations of the different Varieties, drawn from Life by HARRISON WEIR, and printed in Colours by LEIGHTON Brothers; and numerous Woodcuts. Imperial 8vo, half-bound, price 21s.

The Standard of Excellence in Exhibition Poultry. By W. B. TEGETMEIER, F.Z.S. Fcap., cloth, 2s. 6d.

GEORGE ROUTLEDGE & SONS'

NATURAL HISTORY, *continued.*

Pigeons. By W. B. TEGETMEIER, F.Z.S., Assisted by many Eminent Fanciers. With 27 Coloured Plates, drawn from Life by HARRISON WEIR, and printed by LEIGHTON Brothers; and numerous Woodcuts. Imperial 8vo, half-bound, 10s. 6d.

The Homing or Carrier Pigeon: Its History, Management, and Method of Training. By W. B. TEGETMEIER, F.Z.S. 1s. boards.

My Feathered Friends. Containing Anecdotes of Bird Life, more especially Eagles, Vultures, Hawks, Magpies, Rooks, Crows, Ravens, Parrots, Humming Birds, Ostriches, &c., &c. By the Rev. J. G. WOOD. With Illustrations by HARRISON WEIR. Cloth gilt, 3s. 6d.

British Birds' Eggs and Nests. By the Rev. J. C. ATKINSON. With Original Illustrations by W. S. COLEMAN, printed in Colours. Fcap., cloth, gilt edges, price 3s. 6d.

The Angler Naturalist. A Popular History of British Freshwater Fish. By H. CHOLMONDELEY PENNELL. Post 8vo, 3s. 6d.

British Conchology. A Familiar History of the MOLLUSCS of the British Isles. By G. B. SOWERBY. With 20 Pages of Coloured Plates, embracing 150 subjects. Cloth, 5s.

The Calendar of the Months. Giving an Account of the Plants, Birds, and Insects that may be expected each Month. With 100 Illustrations. Cloth gilt, 3s. 6d.; Cheap Edition, 2s.

White's Natural History of Selborne. New Edition. Edited by Rev. J. G. WOOD, with above 200 Illustrations by W. HARVEY. Fcap. 8vo, cloth, 3s. 6d.

Dogs and their Ways. Illustrated by numerous Anecdotes from Authentic Sources. By the Rev. CHARLES WILLIAMS. With Illustrations. Fcap. 8vo, cloth, 3s. 6d.

Sagacity of Animals. With 60 Engravings by HARRISON WEIR. Small 4to, 3s. 6d.

The Young Naturalist. By Mrs. LOUDON. 16mo, cloth, Illustrated, 1s. 6d.

The Child's First Book of Natural History. By Miss BOND. With 100 Illustrations. 16mo, cloth, 1s. 6d.

The Common Objects of the Country. By the Rev. J. G. WOOD. With Illustrations by COLEMAN, containing 150 of the "Objects" beautifully printed in Colours. Cloth, gilt edges, price 3s. 6d.
Also a CHEAP EDITION, price 1s., in fancy boards, with Plain Plates.

Common British Beetles. By the Rev. J. G. WOOD, M.A. With Woodcuts and Twelve pages of Plates of all the Varieties, beautifully printed in Colours by EDMUND EVANS. Fcap. 8vo, cloth, gilt edges, price 3s. 6d.

Westwood's (Professor) British Butterflies and their Transformations. With numerous Illustrations, beautifully Coloured by Hand. Imperial 8vo, cloth. 12s. 6d.

BOOKS ON NATURAL HISTORY, &c.

NATURAL HISTORY, *continued.*

British Butterflies. Figures and Descriptions of every Native Species, with an Account of Butterfly Life. With 71 Coloured Figures of Butterflies, all of exact life-size, and 67 Figures of Caterpillars, Chrysalides, &c. By W. S. COLEMAN. Fcap., cloth gilt, price 3s. 6d.
*** A CHEAP EDITION, with plain Plates, fancy boards, price 1s.

The Common Moths of England. By the Rev. J. G. WOOD, M.A. 12 Plates printed in Colours, comprising 100 objects. Cloth, gilt edges. 3s. 6d.
*** A CHEAP EDITION, with plain Plates, boards, 1s.

British Entomology. Containing a Familiar and Technical Description of the Insects most common to the localities of the British Isles. By MARIA E. CATLOW. With 16 pages of Coloured Plates. Cloth, 5s.

Popular Scripture Zoology. With Coloured Illustrations. By MARIA E. CATLOW. Cloth, 5s.

The Common Objects of the Sea-Shore. With Hints for the Aquarium. By the Rev. J. G. WOOD. The FINE EDITION, with the Illustrations by G. B. SOWERBY, beautifully printed in Colours. Fcap. 8vo, cloth, gilt edges, 3s. 6d.
*** Also, price 1s., a CHEAP EDITION, with the Plates plain.

British Crustacea: A Familiar Account of their Classification and Habits. By ADAM WHITE, F.L.S. 20 Pages of Coloured Plates, embracing 120 subjects. Cloth, 5s.

The Fresh-Water and Salt-Water Aquarium. By the Rev. J. G. WOOD, M.A. With 11 Coloured Plates, containing 126 Objects. Cloth, 3s. 6d.
A CHEAP EDITION, with plain Plates, boards, 1s.

The Aquarium of Marine and Fresh-Water Animals and Plants. By G. B. SOWERBY, F.L.S. With 20 Pages of Coloured Plates, embracing 120 subjects. Cloth, 5s.

FLOWERS, PLANTS, AND GARDENING.

Gardening at a Glance. By GEORGE GLENNY. With Illustrations. Fcap. 8vo, gilt edges, 3s. 6d.

Roses, and How to Grow Them. By J. D. PRIOR. Coloured Plates. Cloth gilt, 3s. 6d.
*** A CHEAP EDITION, with plain Plates, fancy boards, 1s. 6d.

Garden Botany. Containing a Familiar and Scientific Description of most of the Hardy and Half-hardy Plants introduced into the Flower Garden. By AGNES CATLOW. 20 Pages of Coloured Plates, embracing 65 Illustrations. 5s.

ROUTLEDGE'S POCKET LIBRARY.

IN MONTHLY VOLUMES.

Cut or uncut edges, 1s.; *Cloth, uncut edges with gilt tops,* 1s. 6d.
Paste grain, 2s. 6d.

"A series of beautiful little books, tastefully bound."—*Times.*
"Beautifully printed and tastefully bound."—*Saturday Review.*
"Deserves warm praise for the taste shown in its production. The Library' ought to be very popular."—*Athenæum.*

---

1. BRET HARTE'S POEMS.
2. THACKERAY'S PARIS SKETCH BOOK.
3. HOOD'S COMIC POEMS.
4. DICKENS'S CHRISTMAS CAROL.
5. POEMS BY OLIVER WENDELL HOLMES.
6. WASHINGTON IRVING'S SKETCH BOOK.
7. MACAULAY'S LAYS OF ANCIENT ROME.
8. THE VICAR OF WAKEFIELD.
9. HOOD'S SERIOUS POEMS.
10. THE COMING RACE. By LORD LYTTON.
11. THE BIGLOW PAPERS.
12. MANON LESCAUT.
13. LONGFELLOW'S SONG OF HIAWATHA.
14. STERNE'S SENTIMENTAL JOURNEY.
15. DICKENS'S CHIMES.

www.ingramcontent.com/pod-product-compliance
Lightning Source LLC
Chambersburg PA
CBHW030802230426
43667CB00008B/1021